IMPROVISATION

its nature and practice in music

DEREK BAILEY

DA CAPO PRESS

A MEMBER OF THE PERSEUS BOOKS GROUP

Library of Congress Cataloging in Publication Data

Bailey, Derek.
  Improvisation: its nature and practice in music / Derek Bailey.
    p.   cm.
  Originally published: Ashborune, England: Moorland Pub. in association
with Incus Records, c1980.
  Includes bibliographical references and index.
   ISBN-10: 0-306-80528-6   ISBN-13: 978-0-306-80528-8
  1. Improvisation (Music). 2. Music—Performance—History. I. Title.
ML430.7.B25 1993   93-24899
781.3′6—dc20   CIP

First published in the United Kingdom in 1992 by
The British Library National Sound Archive

First published in the United States of America in 1993
by Da Capo Press, supplemented with photographs.

Published by Da Capo Press, Inc.
A Member of the Perseus Books Group

Manufactured in the United States of America

for K

CONTENTS

Author's Note

This book is an account by practicing musicians from various idioms of their use of improvisation, its place in music and their speculations on its nature. The widespread presence of improvisation in music, combined with a scarcity of documentation concerning it, means that any single volume will inevitably be selective. This is an attempt to cover the practice of improvisation in the main areas in which it is found and to reveal those features and characteristics common to all improvisation.

The book is divided into sections ranging from the traditional uses of improvisation (in Indian music, Flamenco and Baroque music) through its uses in church organ playing, in Jazz and in Rock, its relationship to its audience, its relationship to recording, its uses in the classroom and some of the recent developments involving improvisation in contemporary Western composition. It concludes with an examination of some aspects of the recent rise of free improvisation and the correspondences found between all types of improvisation.

Acknowledgements

The number of people who have helped me with the book from its inception through its various stages and revisions is countless. Primarily, I am indebted to all the musicians whose words I quote in the book. They are the book. But I would also like to thank all those musicians whose ideas and words appear without acknowledgement, passages in the book which derive from conversations held with many players over many years.

Among those who helped in a variety of other ways, I have particular reasons to thank Alistair Bamford, Mick Beck, Karen Brookman, Peter Butler, Janice Christianson, Chris Clark, George Clinton, Mandy Davidson, Martin Davidson, John Fordham, Charles Fox, Laurent Goddet, Henry Kaiser, Rudy Koopmans, Frank Long, Paul Lytton, Ulla Lytton, Michael Oliver, Peter Riley, Marion Rout, Beryl Towns and Paul Wilson.

My thanks also to Harcourt Films and Channel 4 Television for permission to use certain quotations from the series of TV films based on the earlier edition of this book. Particularly, I am indebted to the director, Jeremy Marre. His perception of the social and spiritual powers of improvisation lead me to a greater understanding of its universal significance.

Introduction

Improvisation enjoys the curious distinction of being both the most widely practised of all musical activities and the least acknowledged and understood. While it is today present in almost every area of music, there is an almost total absence of information about it. Perhaps this is inevitable, even appropriate. Improvisation is always changing and adjusting, never fixed, too elusive for analysis and precise description; essentially non-academic. And, more than that, any attempt to describe improvisation must be, in some respects, a misrepresentation, for there is something central to the spirit of voluntary improvisation which is opposed to the aims and contradicts the idea of documentation.

My purpose in undertaking such an unlikely project as, firstly, instigating a series of radio programmes in which practising musicians from different idioms discussed their use of improvisation, and then assembling a book combining these programmes and further discussions with these and other players, was to show the significance of improvisation through the experience of those who use it. My feeling was that there was an important part of improvisation not easily indicated or conveyed by its results, a part which perhaps only those involved in doing it seemed to be able to appreciate or comprehend. This suspicion arose mainly as a result of the almost total absence of comment concerning improvisation and the hopeless misconceptions usually expressed in the comment which does occur.

Defined in any one of a series of catchphrases ranging from 'making it up as he goes along' to 'instant composition', improvisation is generally viewed as a musical conjuring trick, a doubtful expedient, or even a vulgar habit. So in this book the intention is to present the views on improvisation of those who use it and know it.

Obviously this is not intended as a history of improvisation, a task which, if it were ever attempted, would be a vast and probably endless undertaking. Even about its presence in Occidental music, the most inhospitable area for improvisation, E.T.Ferand in his *Improvisation in Nine Centuries of Western Music* can write: 'This joy in improvising while singing and playing is evident in almost all phases of music history. It was always a powerful force in the creation of new forms and every historical study that confines itself to the practical or theoretical sources that have come down to us in writing or in print, without taking into account the improvisational element in living musical practice, must of necessity present an incomplete, indeed a distorted picture. For there is scarcely a single field in music that has remained unaffected by improvisation, scarcely a single musical technique or form of composition that did not originate in improvisatory practice or was not essentially influenced by it. The whole history of the development of music is accompanied by manifestations of the drive to improvise.'

So the omissions, those musics which have to be excluded in order to avoid the book assuming encyclopedic proportions, would make an extensive list. It would include many parts of Islamic music (notably Persian *gusheh*), the blues, Turkish music, many African musics, the Polynesian 'variable' musics[1] and all the many forms of vocal improvisation found in settings as culturally different as the Presbyterian chapels of Stornoway[2] and the markets and bazaars of Cairo. Those and many other forms of music involving the use of improvisation are not here.

However, it did become increasingly clear during my contacts with different musicians and their musics that the main characteristics of improvisation could be discerned in all its appearances and roles. What could be said about improvisation in one area could be said about it in another. I hope I have managed to avoid doing that. I have tried, in fact, to use the different sections not only to present an account of improvisation in that area or idiom but to highlight a characteristic most obviously demonstrated by that area. For instance, the section on Indian music examines the usual method of learning to improvise, Flamenco deals with improvisation and authenticity, the chapters on church organ playing present something of the scholastic attitude to improvisation, and so on.

The musics covered here have been chosen simply because I had the opportunity to talk to an active practitioner from each of those fields. I couldn't imagine a meaningful consideration of improvisation from anything other than a practical and a personal point of view. For there is no general or widely held theory of improvisation and I would have thought it self-evident that improvisation has no existence outside of its practice. Among improvising musicians there is endless speculation about its nature but only an academic would have the temerity to mount a theory of improvisation. And even they can run into serious difficulties. Ella Zonis in her book *Classical Persian Music*, after noting that 'Persian music theorists, considering improvisation to be intuitive, do not consider it in their writings', ignores the warning and plunges in. 'A further obstacle in this area is the readily apparent discrepancy between

---

1 The procedure of variation is one of the oldest and most persistent of performing principles, being present without interruption from the earliest known musics to the present day. Early vocal and instrumental improvisation, while it might take the form of embellishment, was not used merely to alter what already existed but as a means of celebrating the act of music-making. It was an end in itself - the means of expression open to the performer. The composition stood or fell on whether or not it provided a good vehicle for improvisation.

2 The collective improvisation by the congregations of these chapels has been described as 'elaborate melismata around an extremely slow moving metrical psalm tune; an astonishing sound, but almost impossible to learn. One has to unlearn the tempered scale to begin with, to say nothing of one's sense of what is harmonically proper'. (Michael Oliver in a letter to the author).

the theory of practice and the practice of practice. Not infrequently, after a lengthy interview regarding performance practices a performer will illustrate the aspects of practice he has just described by playing something entirely different from what he has just said ought to be played. One must realise from the beginning that in Persian music there is no 'always', for no rule or custom is inviolable.' After examining the various structures and constituents in Persian music she later concludes: 'After considering all these procedures, however, we must admit that the performer is not bound by them. For, in Persian music, the essential factors in a performance are the feeling of a player and those of his audience. At the actual time of performance, the musician does not calculate the procedures that will guide his playing. Rather he plays from a level of consciousness somewhat removed from the purely rational... Under these conditions the player performs not according to the "theory of practice", but intuitively, according to the "practice of practice", wherein the dictates of traditional procedures are integrated with his immediate mood and emotional needs.' I hope it will be adequate if I refer to the 'practice of practice' as practice. In any event, that is what this book is mainly about.

There are no so-called 'musical examples' quoted. Transcription, it seems to me, far from being an aid to understanding improvisation, deflects attention towards peripheral considerations. In fact there is very little technical description of any kind, simply because almost all the musicians I spoke to chose to discuss improvisation mainly in 'abstract' terms. In fact there was a commonly held suspicion that a close technical approach was, for this subject, uninformative. In general, intuitive descriptions were preferred and, as Thomas Clifton says: 'The question is not whether the description is subjective, objective, biased or idiosyncratic, but very simply is whether or not the description says something significant about the intuited experience so that the experience itself becomes something from which we can learn and in so doing learn about the object of that experience as well... No one is saying that any particular intuitive description, taken as true, is the whole truth. Intuitive descriptions erect their structures very much in the same way that scientific descriptions do: slowly, methodically with frequent erasures and backtracking. Both kinds of description are concerned with intersubjective confirmation.'3

I have used the terms 'idiomatic' and 'non-idiomatic' to describe the two main forms of improvisation. Idiomatic improvisation, much the most widely used, is mainly concerned with the expression of an idiom - such as jazz, flamenco or baroque - and takes its identity and motivation from that idiom.

3 From 'Some comparisons between intuitive and scientific descriptions of music'. Thomas Clifton in *Journal of Music Theory*.

Non-idiomatic improvisation has other concerns and is most usually found in so-called 'free' improvisation and, while it can be highly stylised, is not usually tied to representing an idiomatic identity. I have also followed what seems to be the usual practice in writings about 'straight' music, of treating the contemporary as a special, quite segregated musical activity. Here one finds 'specialists' in 'new' music as though music, in order to be normal and unspecialised, has to be a sort of sonic archaeology.

The word improvisation is actually very little used by improvising musicians. Idiomatic improvisors, in describing what they do, use the name of the idiom. They 'play flamenco' or 'play jazz'; some refer to what they do as just 'playing'. There is a noticeable reluctance to use the word and some improvisors express a positive dislike for it. I think this is due to its widely accepted connotations which imply that improvisation is something without preparation and without consideration, a completely ad hoc activity, frivolous and inconsequential, lacking in design and method. And they object to that implication because they know from their own experience that it is untrue. They know that there is no musical activity which requires greater skill and devotion, preparation, training and commitment. And so they reject the word, and show a reluctance to be identified by what in some quarters has become almost a term of abuse. They recognise that, as it is generally understood, it completely misrepresents the depth and complexity of their work. But I have chosen to retain that term throughout this book; firstly because I don't know of any other which could effectively replace it, and secondly because I hope that we, the other contributors and myself, might be able to redefine it.

Introduction to revised edition

The difference between the present musical climate and that of the mid-1970s, when this book was first written, could hardly be greater. Most surveys of the intervening decade and a half tend to be lamentations on the galloping artistic cowardice, shrivelled imaginations and self-congratulatory philistinism which typified the period. Other assessors, applauding the strenuous efforts evident in all areas of music to be more 'accessible', speak of a Golden Age. Either way, and significant as they are, the changes that have taken place seem to have made very little difference to improvisation. Transient musical fashion, of course, is unlikely to have any effect on something as fundamental as the nature of improvisation but even in its practice improvisation seems to have been, if at times diverted, as prevalent and irrepressible as ever.

Essential changes to the book, then, were only rarely necessary and revision has mainly taken the form of additions; new voices appearing, some for no more than a single remark, others in extended interviews.

Turning once again from improvising to writing about improvisation was done reluctantly; they are very different activities, it seems to me, and not always compatible. Writing did provide, however, the opportunity to look at the whole thing again through other peoples' eyes, an instructive experience and one intensified this time because I was simultaneously working on a series of TV films based on the earlier edition of this book. That brought its own revelations, as much about television as about improvisation, and while not everything covered in the programmes is of relevance here - TV making its own highly specialised demands - a number of quotations from the discussions held around and during filming are included. Most useful, though, was the opportunity once again to make contact with some of the endlessly various approaches towards improvisation and to be able to further draw on the wealth of insight and practical experience available in virtually all musics as testimony to this bedrock of musical creativity.

Derek Bailey, London, September 1991

INDIAN MUSIC

(1)

Hindustani (North Indian) and Carnatic (South Indian) music are usually considered as two quite distinct musical areas with differences in nomenclature, style and musical grammar. The division in many ways reflects the different cultural and political history of the two areas: South India with its relatively undisturbed Hindu culture producing a music very heavily tied to tradition, conservative in outlook, proud of its rigorous conformity to Sanscrit texts, and earlier saint/composers; Hindustani music, coming from an area which has seen 4000 years of almost continuous invasion and migration beginning with the Aryans and finishing, hopefully, with the English, naturally enough reflects the syntheses it has undergone and is less restricted by inherited convention, although a marked respect for tradition is a prominent part of all Indian music. One effect of this division is that there is a much heavier emphasis on improvisation to be found in Hindustani than in Carnatic music. And the type of attitude customarily associated with improvisation – experimental, tolerant of change, with an interest in development – is much more readily found in the music of the North than that of the South. But in practice, the presence of improvisation is of central importance to all Indian music.

One of the effects of the collision between the Islamic and Hindu cultures occurring in Northern India was to produce a music of a less specifically religious nature than that in the South. A shifting of attention from the traditional texts to the more purely musical side leads to a less rigid, more adventurous attitude in Hindustani music. But historically and theoretically, all Indian music is embedded in the spiritual life of the country. The principles of the music are spiritual principles, the laws of the music are spiritual laws and their authority is of a religious nature. Aesthetics and devotional thinking are inextricably connected. A history of Indian music is largely a catalogue of Hindu and Muslim saints, their teachings and their deeds; a book of musical theory is indistinguishable from a book of religious instruction and although there is a large body of literature concerning the music there is an almost complete absence of systematised, purely musical theory.

The implications and effects of this on the spiritual life of the musician must, of course, be great, and could certainly be considered as belonging within the scope of the subject of this book but it seems to me that one of the

1

most striking advantages that this background has to confer on the Indian musician is of a secular nature. What he is saved from is the burden of having his music constantly monitored by a self-appointed theoretical authority of doubtful utility and, as regards the business of actually playing the music, he is left with enormous practical freedom. In short, the purely theoretical advice he receives is almost entirely of an aesthetic not technical nature. For the development of his musicianship the student in Indian music is left with no alternative but to find practical instruction from a performing musician and, with guidance from his master, to pursue his own personal development and musical self-sufficiency.

* * *

The framework within which improvisation takes place in Indian music is the *raga*, a variable framework. The basic intervals used, the *sruti* and the *svara*, and the rhythmic cycle, the *tala*, are also variable. Consequently, the main raw materials used by the Indian musician are of an unfixed, malleable nature. Improvisation for him is a fact of musical life.

THE SRUTI

In Sanscrit meaning 'to hear', the sruti is the smallest interval used and is considered the most important single element in Indian music. Its exact size is elusive. The octave in Indian music is divided into seven main, unequal units called svaras. The sruti is the subdivision of the svara and its relation to the svara can be $2:1$, $3:1$ or $4:1$, that is, a sruti can be a half or a third or a quarter of the svara, an interval which itself does not have a clearly defined size. The octave, however, does have an exact size and there are 22 srutis to an octave. Again these divisions are not equal.

Arguing about the exact size of the sruti, in any of its versions, seems to have been one of the main tasks of the theorist in this music for over 2000 years. In practice it is clear that a micro-tonal music which is often played on instruments using low-tensioned strings, where most small movement is by glissandi, means that the exact size of the sruti is in many instances purely a matter of personal choice, a choice depending on the musician's knowledge, experience and instinct. The difference between one raga and another *can* be decided by the size of one sruti, but in practice this is always judged in the context of the raga being played, judged in relation to a svara, and judged aurally. But srutis, too, can be considered as the element which guarantees the basic variability of the music; a constant shifting to 'sharpness' or to 'flatness'. The precise opposite of the tempered scale.

Since the arrival on the scene of the Western musicologist the debate about the sruti has intensified. One French scholar, after awesome research, concluded that there were 24, not 22, srutis to the octave. I found an adequate description of the importance and function of the sruti in the work of two Indian writers who were largely unconcerned with precise measurements and exact labels. R.Srinivasan in *Facets of Indian Culture*, writes: 'It is the use of these very short intervals that makes the individuality of the Indian system...the spirit of a Raga or a melody-type is best expressed through the use of these minute divisions of the scale. The expertness of a musician depends to a large extent on his capacity to use them so as to add to the richness and sweetness of his songs.' For a more 'technical' description Shri N.M.Adyonthaya in his *Melody Music of India* offers that 'a further explanation of the basis of the srutis may be found in the audio phenomenon that when two notes of the same pitch are struck simultaneously and one of them is raised gradually higher and higher in pitch relationship or pitch ratio, one of them serving as a basic note of reference, the ear responds and tolerates at certain definite points and there are 22 such points at each of which the degree of tolerance, consonance or dissonance is varying. These 22 points have been the basis of the 22 srutis of Indian music from time immemorial.'

THE SVARA

The seven unequal and variable divisions of the octave, usually compared to a scale, have been more accurately described as the molecular structure of the raga. Although they provide the main tonal points, their identity is not established primarily by their relationship to a tonic and their use is not step-like or sequential. One of the meanings of 'svara' is 'self-sufficient'.

The svara and the sruti form the two basic pitch divisions in Indian music – a music which is, in the Western sense, non-harmonic. The notes relate to each other purely by their continuity and their juxtaposition. A svara is selected and used as a centre around which melodic activity can take place. Most of this activity is in srutis acting as satellites of the svara. The whole of the activity can take place over a continuous drone or fundamental. If a singer is taking part in the performance the drone, or *shadja*, is chosen by the singer and all the instruments tune to that. If there is no singer any player of a melody instrument will choose it.

THE TALA

The tala, which in Sanscrit means the palm of the hand, is the rhythmic cycle over which the second part of the raga is played and is treated mainly as a base for rhythmic variations of fixed metrical length, for example 16, 12, or 8 *matra* (beats); the sub-division of this cycle can become quite complex. Although there are probably over one hundred tala available to the Indian musician there are only about a dozen in general use. The tala is, of course, an integral part, one of the main characteristics, of Indian music but of more importance rhythmically is the *laya*.

THE LAYA

An important part of all idiomatic improvisation is using the 'feel' of the rhythm, the forward movement sense as opposed to the mathematical understanding of the rhythm. In Indian music this is the laya. Usually described as the overall tempo of a piece, it is much more than that. It is its rhythmic impetus, its pulse. The musician who displays an exceptional rhythmical 'feel', whose work has great rhythmic facility and ease, is described as 'having a good laya'. The origin of the word is connected with the Hindu belief in the 'all-embracing comprehensive rhythm of the universe as personified in Shiva, Lord of the Dance'.

The vocabulary of Western classical music contains no equivalent for laya, either being incapable of recognising its existence or preferring to ignore it. Probably the terms encountered in the description of space and energy serve better: continuum, kinetic, dynamic, equivalence, ballistic, centrifugal. Or – like those coined in Western improvisation: groove, swing, rock, ride – words of sexual derivation. The Indians say: 'The laya is the father and the sruti is the mother of the raga.'

The framework within which these elements are working, the raga, is as adaptable and as malleable as they are; not in any way imprecise or unclear in its intentions and requirements, but having the strength and resourcefulness to adapt to any musical direction.

THE RAGA

Until its performance the raga is unformed. It is a set of ingredients all of which are themselves variable and out of which the musician must fashion his performance, his interpretation of these elements. The elements that can be fixed, such as the *sthaya*, the first statement of any melody which might be used at the beginning of the *gat*, and some of the decorative phrases (*gamakas*) are used voluntarily and, if used, the placing and phrasing is chosen at the moment of performance. As with most of the terms used in Indian music there is an ambiguity about the raga which makes a precise definition always, in some respects, misleading. But one can make a generalised description. It is, firstly, an ascending and descending series of svaras, a specific collection of notes which do not, on their own, establish the identity of the raga; one particular row of svaras can be common to more than one raga. The distinction might be in how the svaras are treated, how they are approached, how they are ordered or grouped, how they are left, which svara is selected for emphasis (*vadi*).

The raga is also the framework within which the musician improvises. It is divided into two halves. The first, the *alapa*, forms an out-of-tempo slow introduction. The second, the gat, is played over the tala, the rhythmic cycle, and the characteristic material of the raga is treated in various standard ways.

The two halves are further sub-divided but there are many versions of how many sub-divisions there should be. However it is fairly standard in practice that the following sequences take place:

THE ALAPA

The svaras to be used are established and the dominating notes selected. At this point there is no tala. Melodic patterns are established and the pace quickens. A pulse is introduced but no tala.

THE GAT

The raga melody is stated and the tala introduced. There is movement into a higher register, the introduction of set decorative pieces, and a concentration on the rhythmic properties of the performance. Dialogue between the performers increases in intensity and pace.

This outline is probably used, wholly or in abbreviation, in most performances but my impression is that there is no shortage of exceptions.

* * *

So a raga provides the material, certain standard ways of treating the material, and the framework for the performance. There are also many decorations and graces which are standardised. But the whole thing is in flux, achieving its final state only at the moment of performance. One further point, something common to most improvised music, is that different constituents do not have obvious hierarchical values. Anything which can be considered as decoration, for instance, is not in some way subservient to that which it decorates. The most powerful expression of the identity of a piece might be in the smallest details.

Finally, concerning the raga, O.C.Gangoly in *Ragas and Raginis* writes: 'A raga is more than its physical form...its body. It has a soul which comes to dwell and inhabit the body. In the language of Indian poetics this soul – this principle – is known as the Rasa, or flavour, its sentiment, its impassioned feeling.'

* * *

Representing Indian music in the programmes was Viram Jasani. Born in Jaipur in North India where he studied with Imrat Khan, younger brother of Vilyat Khan, Viram Jasani now lives in England. He gave me the following account of the raga. As he talked he played the sitar, demonstrating the different points he was making. With him was the tabla player Esmail Sheikh. Quite a simple description, it is a succinct account of the essentials involved, even without the musical examples. The points at which these took place are indicated in the text by ellipses.

When we start a performance of the raga we start very slowly. We play what is called alapa. And the purpose of alapa is to explore the melodic possibilities within that raga, which has nothing to do with rhythm or style. And the first thing we do is to establish the keynote... This can be done with a drone or just by playing a phrase up the keynote... Then the improvisations take place in the lower register... And here you do in fact apply a simple mathematical process. But not all of these possibilities may be allowed in the raga. You've got to decide which ones are allowed and which ones to play and how to play them. And you take out one note...and concentrate on that one note... And in this way you work your way up the scale. The whole thing is then repeated on the basis of a rhythm created, in this case on the sitar, on the drone... And concentrating on this note...and building up my phrases to end on that point... And you pick out each note in this scale as you go up the scale and your phrases are created and improvised around each particular note, and this is why it takes such a long time, perhaps, to play a good performance. Now all this is done without any rhythm whatever. Where the drums come in, and this is where improvisation perhaps begins to get a little less, is where one has a fixed composition – one can either make up a composition or you can play a traditional tune from your style of music; one which your teacher is famous for, perhaps. And this tune may have a certain length in time, and there is an emphasised point in that tune which corresponds to the emphasised point in the time cycle. And we both meet on that point... And while I repeat this tune over and over I am maintaining this time cycle, which leaves the tabla player, the drummer, free to improvise, while the time cycle is still being maintained. If we just have an example of him playing and he will come back and end his improvisations at the same point of emphasis... Then he maintains the cycle and I am free to improvise, and we alternate; and this is where one tends to play much faster phrases, which may seem a contradiction, to its slower atmosphere. But that's Indian music. Full of contradiction, I am afraid.

6

INDIAN MUSIC

The learning process in improvisation is invariably difficult to detect. Although a large number of books and courses offering instruction and advice on how to improvise are available it seems impossible to find a musician who has actually learned to improvise from them. The great majority of these studies concern themselves either with organ improvisation, the earliest of which appeared over 200 years ago, or conventional jazz. And the instruction offered usually concerns the manipulation of scalar and harmonic ingredients in those particular styles. What they have to say is, in most cases, helpful for an appreciation of those idioms and, naturally, an understanding of the idiom is essential in order to improvise in it. But a discourse which concerns itself exclusively with pitch relationships – melodic or harmonic – can say practically nothing about that which is essentially to do with improvisation.

In the face of the possibility that no improvisor anywhere has ever learned to improvise from a book or other documentary source, the argument usually offered to support the publication of these manuals is that while 'great' players can somehow suddenly appear fully endowed with every necessary skill, more ordinary players have to find more ordinary means. The truth is probably that improvisation is learned – perhaps acquired would be a better word – in pretty much the same way by everybody who is lucky enough to stumble on the right method. An ability to improvise can't be forced and it depends, firstly, on an understanding, developed from complete familiarity, of the musical context in which one improvises, or wishes to improvise. As this understanding develops so the ability to improvise can develop. The important thing is to have an objective, the recognition of which can be intuitive, so strongly desired as to be almost a mania. In idiomatic improvisation this objective is usually represented by an admired player whose performance one wishes to emulate. In the early stages this admiration is most useful if it takes the form of unquestioning idolatry. Alain Danielou, writing of the traditional method of learning in South-East Asia, says: 'In this sort of personal instruction artistic training precedes the technical. The pupil is in constant contact with the work of art in its most developed form and he is conscious of the goal which he should eventually attain: the content of the music is never separated from its form.' Later the path to musical self-development comes through increasing confidence and the inevitable increase in critical awareness.

Most musicians learn to improvise by accident; or by a series of observed accidents; by trial and error. And there is of course an appropriateness about this method, a natural correspondence between improvisation and empiricism. Learning improvisation is a practical matter: there is no exclusively theoretical side to improvisation. Appreciating and understanding how improvisation works is achieved through the failures and successes involved in attempting to do it. Indian music with its long complex relationship between teacher and pupil has the only methodology or system which acknowledges these basic characteristics of improvisation.

Viram Jasani described to me how improvisation 'arrived' during his years of study.

The time that we spend with a Guru is purely spent in trying to understand the framework in which Indian music is set. And a Guru doesn't, or your teacher doesn't, really tell you how to improvise. That is purely up to the student to gain by experience and to intuit the various methods of playing the music. What he directly learns from his teacher is the framework in which improvisation or performance of Indian music takes place. But the teacher in Indian music is not usually an academic, he's not a theoretician, therefore a good teacher is able to show you and give you guidelines as to how to perform Indian classical music. He gives you the scope and the field in which to gain your experience and if you're a good student you take advantage of this opportunity that he gives you and then it becomes something that one develops on one's own.

Could Viram Jasani be more specific about his teacher's methods and could he recall his first attempts at improvising?

It's difficult to pinpoint a particular time when you start improvising. What happens is that your teacher, when he's in the mood to teach you a particular raga, won't say to you, 'this is the scalic structure of the raga and these are the notes used in that raga' – what he will do is to play to you and tell you to listen and perhaps ask you to imitate certain phrases that he is playing. And gradually, after hearing him do this several times, what you do is to acquire a feeling for that raga and you can immediately recognise it when it's played by other musicians or by your teacher again. And so you start playing those phrases and eventually you get to the stage where you don't repeat the phrases your teacher has taught you, you start creating your own different phrases within that raga. And you intuit when you're playing a phrase which is out of context, out of that framework. In other words, when you learn a raga you are really learning something which is very abstract and you don't learn a raga in terms of its tonal content.

Viram Jasani demonstrated what he meant.

I'll play a few phrases within this raga, without any direct...implication as to how one actually improvises in this raga but just to demonstrate to you how to feel for the raga and then I'll at one point deliberately play something which you will automatically recognise as not part of the raga – just to show the power of the raga and how you immediately realise that something is not correct...

This almost uses the same intonation...one note is incorrect...that is, as you would say, the natural seventh, which should have been the flattened seventh. Now your teacher doesn't tell you that these are the notes that you use so that you know which ones not to use. What he does is to play you phrases and play you the general...give you an idea of the gait of the raga...how it should be played. There are plenty of...what we call meend or slides, between notes. And there is more emphasis...on the lower notes in the lower register. This all goes to make up an atmosphere of sobriety, of austerity. But ultimately I don't think musicians think in terms like these. They are musicians and they think of the feeling they have for the notes, and the feeling that they derive from the notes.

Because we are learning, if you like, a language of music, it comes naturally to us to think of our own phrases and our own representation of a performance of a raga.

Ours is a very intuitive music, you learn intuitively, the feeling for a raga is acquired intuitively.

I suggested to Viram Jasani that one of the purposes of improvisation might be to intensify the mood of a raga.

That's absolutely right. To bring out the most in that raga. In purely mathematical terms a series of notes can be combined in hundreds of different ways. But it's useless in your improvisation to go through all of these. Theoretically it might be correct but it doesn't allow for the feelings of the raga, it doesn't allow for music.

One has to figure out a way in which the possibilities of that raga will enhance its mood.

And, of course, a raga can be considered a limiting thing. How, after all, do you recognise a raga? Because you recognise certain characteristic features about it. And if you are going to play that raga you can't help but play those characteristic features. So this, perhaps, is not improvisation. But your improvisation comes into play when you are trying to use the information presented to you in terms of musical facts, using your ability, and the experience acquired over the years of practicing that raga, and listening to other people play that raga, to put all this together and create some new phrase or put a new idea within that raga.

9

When asked how he judged the quality of an improvisation, what made one improvisation better than another, Viram Jasani, like most improvising musicians, couldn't offer a formula or a set of rules that one could apply.

It's the combination achieved by: tempo – what's happened before – what's going to come after – the tone of the instrument – the particular tone you bring out of the instrument at that time – the mood created – perhaps a phrase which isn't necessarily new but just put in a different context.

I asked Viram Jasani if there was any deliberate attempt at some sort of evolution in his improvising – whether over the years he was actually trying to move it somewhere.

That is, in fact, how ragas evolve. Because a musician is trying to use whatever liberty he has within the raga to extend the limits of that raga without destroying its basic features. And if you take a raga today and look at it in terms of its history you may find that it has changed considerably. But it is changed not by one performer but by a succession of performers. So the changes are imperceptible over any short period of time. They become part of the raga. I think a raga is a product of time and people playing that raga over a period of time. It's a product of peoples' changing attitudes and tolerances.

Something common to most musics in which improvisation is traditionally found is an absence of any accurate notation system. Curt Sachs in *The Wellsprings of Music* writes: '...music without notation is not limited to scriptless societies. Many ancient notations were merely devised by priests for priests and cantors and some were even kept secret. While in religious music notation had a definite place in order to prevent the present and future generations from breaking sacred traditions, secular music relied on free invention and memory, in Western civilisation as well as those of the East. Notation became indispensible only under the pressure of worked-out polyphony.'

'Written music' in Indian music usually refers to books of music theory (accepted as being quite separate from music practice, the one rarely interfering with the other). Consequently, instruction has to be aural, by rote, and personal. But there are other implications to the lack of written music.

Whether reading music is a disadvantage to an improvisor is a question which gets quite a lot of discussion amongst improvising musicians who work in areas such as popular music, where they might be expected both to improvise and to read music. The argument usually revolves around the point whether the skills and attitudes necessary to be a good sight-reader are, or are not, inhibiting factors when it comes to improvisation. There is an unmistakable suspicion that the acquisition of reading skills in some way has a blunting effect on improvising skills, an acceptance that these are very often two things which do not go together. So, of course, in musics where there isn't an 'accurate' notation system, that possible problem, or distraction, disappears. But more important than the removal of a possible inhibition or contrary discipline from the performer is the fact that the absence of a music writing/reading tradition gets rid of the composer.

Writings of a spiritual and of an aesthetic nature or poems which have inspired musicians are the only types of scripted works which are allowed to influence and affect the Indian performing musician. In practice the only part of the music which might be identified as 'composed music' is the possible use of certain melodies with certain ragas. Written by, or associated with, historic figures of Indian music, usually great performers or religious teachers of the past, their use, once a symbolic act of piety, is now a matter of musical choice. The ragas, the bedrock and stuff of the music, develop and evolve through the type of process described earlier by Viram Jasani. One of the few sustained efforts to deliberately mould or shape the course of the music has been the attempt in recent years to synthesise or combine different ragas. But here again the experiments are carried out by performers and receive their 'tests' in performance.

So, as with all improvisors, there is an assumption by the player that the music is his; his creation, his presentation, his responsibility. I had this exchange with Viram Jasani:

Does the amount of improvisation used increase as you go on? Would it be possible to say that?

I don't understand what you mean when you say 'amount of improvisation used'.

Would you introduce more of your own...

The whole thing is one's own...the whole performance is one's own interpretation on that raga.

Improvisors in all fields often speak of 'my music'. It is not a claim of ownership but a complete personal identification with the music they play. They, 'the musicians', are the embodiment of the music. And in India, where, as Yehudi Mehuhin says, '...music has continued unperturbed through thirty centuries or more, with the even pulse of a river and with the unbroken evolution of a Sequoia tree', the continuance and evolution of their music has throughout the centuries been the successful charge of the improvising performer.

FLAMENCO

The profusion of documentary material, mostly of a contradictory, somewhat ambiguous nature, found in Indian music, is paralleled by an almost total absence of any literature, reliable or otherwise, concerning flamenco. It is possible to find brief accounts of Spanish dance but the music which first accompanied it and then developed into a completely self-sufficient genre has been very little described. The advantages for the performing musician in this situation are numerous. In fact, Debussy, writing about Spanish song, implied that a lack of documentation was of benefit to everyone. 'Fortunate is the country which jealously guards these natural flowers, preserving them from the classico-administrative.' So most of my information has come from musicians who play flamenco. Incidentally, when I checked with them the small amount of documentary evidence I could uncover, they found it contained very little that could be recognised as accurately reflecting the music they played.

My main informant and guide was Paco Peña. One of today's finest flamenco guitarists, he was born in Cordoba, and from the age of twelve has worked professionally; first as an accompanist with a number of dance troupes and then either as a soloist or with his own Flamenco Puro group. In 1972 he gave a recital in the Conservatorio da Musica in Cordoba, becoming the first flamenco guitarist ever to play in a conservatorio in Spain. An event not only of great personal distinction for Paco Peña but a nice indication of the relationship existing between the academic and flamenco music worlds.[1]

Andalucia, the home of flamenco, has, like Northern India, a musical background built up from the influences and cultural remnants left by the various peoples who passed through or settled on its land. Similarly, Andalucia was under Moorish domination for many centuries – Cordoba being at one time the capital of the Western Islamic world. Paco Peña gave me the following account of how flamenco arose from this background.

In the 15th century, many tribes of gypsies found their way into Andalucia as a branch of immigrants who around 1447 entered Spain by Catalonia. They lived mainly in the fields, nomadically, and in poor

---

1 It seems that in 1922 when judging a competition held to assist 'native' performers to enter a Spanish music college, the composer Manuel de Falla used the occasion to advise and instruct the applicants in authenticity, demonstrating yet again the combination of ignorance and arrogance with which high culture usually approaches anything beyond its own narrow territory.

conditions. Traditionally the gypsies were not great poets – hardly surprising considering their circumstances – but they had a remarkable facility for rhythm and music, and in Andalucia they found a rich, colourful folklore of exceptional poetic charm. Unlike other music they had come across elsewhere in Spain, this folklore suited their character and came to form part of their lives. They assimilated it and added something different to it. This 'marriage' gave rise to the phenomenon of Cante Flamenco, neither 'gypsy music' nor Andalucian folklore, but both. So, it can be said without doubt that there are two main elements in flamenco: Andalucia with its old musical background, and the gypsies – without both, flamenco would never have existed.

Nobody knows for certain when it all started because there are very few written records available. The first notice we have is about a singer of seguirillas, Tio Luis el de la Juliana, around 1780. But even that is a little dubious because it was not mentioned until a century later – in 1881 – by Antonio Machado Alvarez ('Demofilo'); in fact the Seguiriya seems to have developed later from another style, Tonas.

There are three main periods in the history of flamenco. From the beginning of the 19th century to 1860 it was part of the life of Andalucian gypsies and poor people who kept it for themselves and never performed outside their communities. From 1860 to 1910 was the era of the 'Cafe Cantantes', special tablaos or places dedicated wholly to flamenco music. Since then flamenco has emerged from its original environment to become known throughout the world.

No evidence exists that guitars were used during the first period. But as flamenco emerged ('Cafes Cantantes'), the guitar, which was already the instrument of Spain, was brought in to accompany and enhance the human voice. Paradoxically, it is the guitar as a solo instrument rather than the singing, which has made flamenco popular, when in fact the guitar, like the dancing, derives all its inspiration from the Cante Jondo – flamenco singing – the purest expression of Andalucian art.

A complete flamenco performance is a group performance with singing, dancing, and instrumental music, and containing possibilities for improvisation by all the participants. Paco Peña outlined the role of the guitarist:

When accompanying, the function of the flamenco guitarist is to help the singer or dancer to bring out the best of his talent. He must create an atmosphere suitable to each piece, and he must provide a good clear rhythm and follow the voice in whatever nuances the singer may bring to it. Also he must colour it by playing falsetas, or very brief melodic sequences between verses. The guitarist is then at the absolute service of the singing and from it he takes all his inspiration.

13

But when playing solo, the guitarist must convey the whole atmosphere of flamenco. The falsetas become much more elaborate and musical to resemble the singing. The rhythm becomes stronger and more elaborate to resemble the 'foot-work' of the dancer.

As in Indian music the framework within which the musician works and the constituents within that framework are variable, receiving their final form only in performance.

The framework in flamenco is referred to as the style and it is the dance style or song. This is distinguished by its *compas*. The compas is the rhythmic unit: a set number of beats with certain accents. This is fixed, but the overall length of the piece and its proportions are alterable at any time. The harmony is common to all styles but its use varies greatly. Usually it consists of the most basic chords, tonic, dominant, and sub-dominant, with, in some styles, the chords on the steps of the Phrygian mode used as 'passing' chords. Additionally, there is a heavily instrumental aspect to the harmony. Many 'mixed' chords are used which obviously have as their source the guitar and its chromatic nature. The selection of chords used may be associated with the style being played, but how they are used is decided largely in performance. Although the harmony will not differ much from performance to performance, what will differ is the time spent with each chord. There is no set sequence length. The harmony changes when the vocal or instrumental embellishments on that chord are completed. Improvisation is in relation to this harmonic vocabulary and in relation to the *falsetas*, or melodic fragments, which constitute the only predetermined melodic material used (although the exact placement or phrasing of the falsetas is never fixed).

There are many styles, almost all with some geographical association and identified by their mood. Each one will be characterised by its own special pace and compas. The four most common, most basic, styles are: *Bulerias, Soleares, Tientos* and *Seguirillas*.

Bulerias is something of an exceptional piece. Very light, playful, often full of quotations, it is a piece in which anything can happen. However the other three have much in common, and the chief of these is Soleares.

One can say that Soleares is the perfect form of Cante Flamenco where beauty and depth of feeling are in harmony. Ever since I remember playing the guitar I remember playing Soleares. It's a very beautiful style – it moves but it's not very fast.

The compas, or rhythmic unit, of the Soleares has 12 beats accented in the following manner: 1 2 3̌ 4 5 6̌ 7 8̌ 9 1̌0 11 1̌2. Everything played must be accommodated within this gait. Whether actually played or not these accents are always felt and expressed.

14

Paco Peña made it clear that the foregoing technical matters were, in his view, of only peripheral significance to the subject we were discussing.

You should understand this: each song or each style of flamenco has a different sound, and what you must do, what you normally do, is to get involved in that sound. There is a kind of mood that you must get into – you must get inside the music. It's an abstract thing. Even if there is no rhythm, you produce something, you see. You move around and you dance.

* * *

For the musical theorist there seems to be no description or evaluation without technical analysis which in turn usually relies on transcription and dissection. For the description – or evaluation – of improvisation, formal technical analysis is useless.

Firstly, it is not possible to transcribe improvisation. There have been some attempts; usually of jazz solos, or organ improvisations and sometimes of 'ethnic' music. Invariably the transcription is into 'standard' musical notation, a system which concerns itself almost exclusively with representing pitch and rhythm within certain conventions. However, most improvisation has scant regard for the niceties of the tempered scale, or for exactly uniform divisions of the 'bar' or beat. Attempts to show its 'deviations' usually take the form of arrows, dots, cent numbers, commas and all sorts of minute adjustments hopefully scattered through the standard notation system. But at the end of a lifetime in which he did an awful lot of transcribing, Curt Sachs wrote: 'We know from bitter experience how unreliable and deadly prejudiced man's senses are, how easily we project into a totally foreign style of music the tempered melody steps and even stressed rhythms of Western tradition and hence, how small is the documentary value of such unverified impressions.' Even when man's senses are supplemented by such devices as the oscillator and the frequency analyser the result is only a more exact picture of the irrelevancies. It still has nothing to say about the forces behind the music making. Transcription might help to establish matters to do with style or material used but those elements which are peculiar to improvisation and to nothing else cannot be documented in this way. But the real indictment of transcription is that in most cases it is used to reduce a performance music to a condition in which it can be examined as if it were composition. When the object of examination is improvisation, transcription, whatever its accuracy, serves only as a misrepresentation.

The improvisors I spoke to, in almost all cases, did not find any sort of technical description adequate. It wasn't that they weren't interested in technical matters. They just did not find them suitable for illuminating improvisation. They finally chose to describe what they wanted to describe in so-called 'abstract' terms. And it became clear that, whatever its deficiencies, this is the best method available. An abstract description of improvisation can achieve, perhaps, a sighting. Close, technical analysis leads elsewhere.

I asked Paco Peña how much the proportions of improvised to non-improvised music in any piece would vary from performance to performance. Would the proportions be the same in each performance or would they vary?

No, they would, in fact, vary very much. Because I don't consider improvisation only to play different notes within a piece. I also consider improvisation to actually change the weight of a piece from one place to another. Change the direction. I mean you might play roughly the same piece and yet because you are feeling quite different, you are producing a completely different piece of music – really and truly.

You ask how much is improvised? Of course it all depends on how inspired you are. In my experience if I feel good technically, funnily enough, if I feel good technically and the conditions are right, I tend to improvise much more. You see – I let myself go – I'm confident. I want to reach other levels, you know.

Later we got back to the same point.

I like to put right something which you said just now – I don't want to be dishonest about it. It seems that you may understand – you may take it – that at the moment when I am playing I am creating a piece of music. This is not so. You know, I don't improvise – and nobody that I know playing flamenco improvises – so much that he is making everything.

I'd say that within a piece you can reach certain heights because you have let yourself improvise, say, a little bit, not too much, but that little bit changes the whole character of the piece, in fact you might change perhaps a quarter of the piece, but that quarter changes the whole character of the whole piece. But I certainly would not say that the whole piece is improvised – anyway in my case it never is completely improvised – but it is true that it can change according to how I feel at the moment.

This seemed to be a fairly common feeling – that the amount altered or added or wholly invented was not of too much significance.

The wonderful thing about this music is that you are completely free. You see, you feel so free because today you are going to play differently from yesterday. You are not tied by a composed piece which you have to play the same but better if you want to improve it. You could play much simpler – the piece could be less complicated, less elaborate and yet more subtle and therefore inspire you. You are so free – and it works both ways. Both ways being that you are completely free to improvise and that you also have the choice not to improvise. You can leave it as it is, simply because it feels better to leave it as it is.

Did Paco Peña make any preparation or do any particular practising for his improvising?

Not specifically for improvising. I think I do prepare to be able, technically, to reach anything I want to reach on the guitar and for that, of course, I do my exercises and so on. But nothing specifically for improvising.

Do you think your improvising might be affected by anything outside flamenco? Do other types of music influence you?

Well, I don't listen to much other music except classical and flamenco. I listen to a lot of classical music, I know a lot of classical musicians, I love classical music and, of course, I take as much benefit from it as I can; and discussing points with other musicians helps me.

But if, shortly before a performance, you heard a recording – Segovia playing Bach, say – might the general air of the piece have any effect on your coming performance?

Oh yes – but for that matter anything which has art in it would have an effect. For example, the way people move – you could see somebody moving gracefully and that inspires you.

Another point I wanted to pursue was the purpose of improvisation. It was obviously essential to flamenco, but why? What did it do?

Being creative within flamenco is essential... You cannot play anybody else's material forever – you've got to make your own otherwise you are just very unhappy...

In order that I get inspired by something I have to hear it very fresh – but I have heard a lot of flamenco, you see. In order that I fulfil myself playing I have to play very well... it's got to be new. If not the rhythm or the notes at least the spirit of it should be new.

This is one of the immediate and direct effects of improvisation. It secures the total involvement of the performer. Better than any other means it provides the possibility for the player to completely identify with the music.

The responsibility to and for the idiom shown by Viram Jasani was the same in Paco Peña. His work served flamenco and flamenco provided a complete framework for his playing. Beyond everything else his main concern was for the authenticity of his music. But authenticity for him did not mean undeviating allegiance to a fixed historical manner transforming the music into a present day dead-letter representation of an earlier time. Improvisation provided the means by which he could maintain authenticity and still have change, freshness and development in the music. And an improvisation was

17

valid in so far as it served that end. I asked Paco Peña what he would do if he played something which interested him but was not characteristically flamenco? He didn't seem particularly worried about the possibility.

The point is that it would be a failure, but not a very unhappy failure. You see it is a failure because I should really be able to resolve what I want to do within the idiom of flamenco.

No idiomatic improvisor is concerned with improvisation as some sort of separate isolated activity. What they are absolutely concerned about is the idiom: for them improvisation serves the idiom and is the expression of that idiom. But it still remains that one of the main effects of improvisation is on the performer, providing him with a creative involvement and maintaining his commitment. So, in these two functions, improvisation supplies a way of guaranteeing the authenticity of the idiom, which also, avoiding the stranglehold of academic authority, provides the motor for change and continuous development.

We have learned from our elders what they had learned from their elders. But we assimilate the music and treat it in our own way, as they did before. Flamenco is not a museum piece but a living developing art form, and as such it allows for the personal interpretation of the artists.

BAROQUE

(1)

The petrifying effect of European classical music on those things it touches – jazz, many folk musics, and all popular musics have suffered grievously in their contact with it – made the prospect of finding improvisation there pretty remote. Formal, precious, self-absorbed, pompous, harbouring rigid conventions and carefully preserved hierarchical distinctions; obsessed with its geniuses and their timeless masterpieces, shunning the accidental and the unexpected: the world of classical music provides an unlikely setting for improvisation.

And yet improvisation played an important part throughout most of its early history. The working out and early practice of Gregorian chant and of polyphony was in both cases largely through improvisation; the 17th century school of organ music was mainly developed through performers' extemporisations, and throughout the 17th and 18th centuries accompaniment both in opera and in concerted chamber music was generally left to be improvised over a figured bass which itself grew out of improvised counterpoint. At the beginning of the baroque period improvised ornamentation extended equally to secular and sacred forms, to the arias of opera and oratorio, to cantatas and 'sacred concertos', to songs and solo vocal pieces of all sorts and it appeared also in the newly rising forms of instrumental music, especially sonatas and concertos. Hardly a single form of vocal or instrumental music of that time is conceivable without some degree of ornamentation, sometimes written down but much more usually added in performance: the *passaggi* of the Italians, the *agréments* of the French, the *graces* of the English and the *glosas* of the Spaniards. Even much later than the baroque period Paganini could write: 'My duties require me to play in two concerts each week and I always improvise with piano accompaniment. I write this accompaniment in advance and work out my theme in the course of the improvisation.'[1]

---

1 The most impressive documentation concerning improvisation that I discovered during my admittedly haphazard researches for this book were the volumes by Ernst T.Ferand. Firstly, *Improvisation in Nine Centuries of Western Music*, which is a comprehensive account of improvised, mainly vocal, decoration edited by Ferand and published in 1961 (Arno Volk Verlag) and also his Die Improvisation in der Musik, Zurich, 1938. There is also a pamphlet, *The Howling in Seconds of the Lombards*, reprinted from the Musical Quarterly, July 1939, in which Ferand touches on uses of improvisation in early European music. Intended mainly as a contribution to a somewhat arcane debate on the 'false' counterpoint alleged to have taken place in the 15th century, the pamphlet contains a couple of references to improvisation, including: 'Instead of the consonances of the fifth and the fourth, the sharpest dissonances – major and minor seconds, ninths, and sevenths – predominate; and, in contrast to the arrangement customary in discant, the main voice (tenor) is in the upper part while the accompanying voice (here called *succentus*) is in the lower part.

The gradual restriction and eventual elimination of improvisation in this music also seems to have taken place over the same period that saw the increasing ascendancy of the orchestral conductor, the composer's proxy. In *Crowds and Power* Elias Canetti likened him to a chief of police. 'The immobility of the audience is as much part of the conductor's design as the obedience of the orchestra. They are under a compulsion to keep still. Until he appears they move about and talk freely among themselves. The presence of the players disturbs no-one; indeed they are scarcely noticed. Then the conductor appears and everyone becomes still. He mounts the rostrum, clears his throat and raises his baton; silence falls. While he is conducting no-one may move and as soon as he finishes they must applaud. All their desire for movement, stimulated and heightened by the music, must be banked up until the end of the work and must then break loose... Presence of mind is among his essential attributes; law-breakers must be curbed instantly. The code of laws, in the form of the score, is in his hands. There are others who have it too and can check the way it is carried out, but the conductor alone decides what the law is and summarily punishes any breach of it... He is the living embodiment of the law, both positive and negative. His hands decree and prohibit. His ears search out profanation.'

* * *

One part of European music where improvisation has achieved, if not survival, at least a sort of embalming is in the re-creation of baroque music. Lionel Salter, the well known harpsichordist and director of baroque ensembles, explained to me where improvisation originally lay in baroque.

Start from the viewpoint that the music as written down was only a kind of memory jogger. It represented a skeleton of what was played, so that a violinist, for example, would expect to have to ornament what was on his part; to that extent there's some improvisation.

When it came to slow movements particularly, of course, you find that the notes written down represent a very bare outline, and people who try and play ... let's say Handel sonatas, strictly according to the text, end up with something at which Handel would probably have laughed uproariously,

(1 cont.) According to Gafori, this remarkable survival of a primitive polyphony was used in the Ambrosian liturgy at solemn vigils in honour of martyrs, at lamentations, and at masses for the dead. In view of this special usage, one may assume that the dissonances mentioned were employed quite deliberately and indeed in improvisatory fashion as 'expressionistic' means for achieving dramatic effects.' The same pamphlet also contains a description of the step from polyphony to a chordal conception of music as it came about in improvised part singing. Apart from the usefulness of his information it really was refreshing to come across a scholar whose approach to improvisation was based on an appreciation and acceptance of its powers, not on an examination of what it didn't do.

because he never expected it to be played cold-bloodedly, just like that. In those days composers expected to perform their own works and sometimes out of sheer lack of time they wouldn't write everything down on paper, they'd just put a thing down to remind themselves that here they were going to do something rather special.

How did they view their improvising? Would they view it as improvisation or as a sort of expediency? Was it a skill they might have developed? Were they conscious of it as a special part of their musicianship?

I don't think they separated it in their own minds at all. It was all part of the performance. If you have a continuo instrument, such as the harpsichord, its function is not merely to fill out the harmony and keep things together, it's much more than that. The continuo player was often the, as it were, conductor for the group. He had to provide a rhythmic spur to the other people. It was a way of integrating all that was going on. The composer wrote simply a bass line, the harmonies were either implicit or he put it down in shorthand by means of the figures, and the keyboard player constructed a part which made musical sense. And this I think is where many people get the wrong impression altogether of continuo playing. It was neither a part to show off how clever you were as a keyboard player, nor simply a dreary series of chords, but it was part of the ensemble, it had to fit in with the general style – with the texture, and act as a stimulus to the other people in the group. It is a two-way thing. The violinists, and the other string players in the group, spurred the harpsichordist on to invent something and vice versa... the harpsichordist might then think of something first and they would follow him.

* * *

In the history of Western European music the baroque period finds its origins in the 16th century and continues, in some form or other, well into the 18th. It was a period remarkable for new developments and innovations. Baroque in its own time was an evolving music, in some ways experimental, the new music of that time.

In all styles of baroque, whatever period, whatever country, improvisation was always present, integrated into both the melodic and harmonic fabric of the music. To decorate, to supplement, to vary, to embellish, to *improve*, as it was often called, was an accepted part of being a performing musician. He would have at his fingertips many standard embellishments and graces, frequently abbreviated when written, or represented by signs, and he would be expected to interpret them with a certain freedom. Couperin: 'What we write is different from what we play.' In many types of performance one of the

21

standard structures used – ABA – always contained one section, the recapitulation of the first section after the contrasting middle section, in which the performer was expected to make the greatest contribution. Singers and violinists were judged on their ability to provide bravura technical displays; the *fioratura* – the heavily decorated phrase or passage – was a feature of any musician's performance. This improvisation was to be found in the essentially melodic side of the music but it was in the realisation of the figured bass – the basso continuo or thorough-bass – that improvisation found its greatest expression and its main opportunities.

Every study of baroque music stresses the importance of the thorough-bass. The years between 1600 and 1750 have been called 'the era of the thorough-bass'. Although capable of great complexity and sophistication, thorough-bass was essentially the transforming of a single note bass harmony into a full and complete accompaniment. J.D.Heinichen wrote in 1728: 'And what actually is the playing of a thorough-bass other than to improvise upon a given bass, the remaining parts of a full harmony?' Of the many books published concerning the realisation of the thorough-bass accompaniment, the first really comprehensive one was *Der General-Bass in der Komposition* from which the above quotation was taken. Written by Johann David Heinichen and published in 1711, a later version, re-written and greatly extended, was published at his own expense in 1728. It is this later edition, running to 960 pages, excluding preface and index, which must be considered as the greatest source book of the period.

His lifespan, 1683 to 1729, covered the high point of the late baroque period. During this time German culture was experiencing the impact of Italian artists in all spheres but particularly in connection with the rise of opera. These were the years in which German music achieved a synthesis of many conflicting national trends, and Heinichen was throughout his career in contact with many of the important musical events of that era, working and studying in three of the great centres of baroque: Leipzig, Venice and Dresden. As an active practitioner, composer and performer, completely involved in the music of the time, Heinichen was probably the ideal man to write on what was essentially a performance music.

The practice of thorough-bass could vary widely – there being distinctions in accompaniment for sacred, operatic, chamber and orchestral styles as well as regional and the main national – Italian and French – variations. The harmony, however, was always indicated by a combination of bass note, numbers and accidentals, a code from which the player would develop his accompaniment. (It is a system with many present day parallels, usually found whenever the emphasis is on practical music-making.)

22

It was the practice during this period to construct and organise chords on an actual, not a theoretical bass, the construction relating to and deriving from the lowest note, not to a theoretical root. In post-baroque period writings[2] references to inversions are found, for example a 2/4/6 construction on a sub-dominant might be referred to as the third inversion of the dominant 7th, but this would never be considered as such by the performer of the time. It would be considered only as a chord constructed on the sub-dominant. Probably this led to some of the subsequent confusion and haggling over doubling. At any event it was normal practice to double up to 4, 5 or 6 parts, and liberties taken with voice leading, inconsistencies in the number of parts, unconventional doubling in chords – all the freedoms taken with harmonic and contrapuntal practices that might repel an unimaginative theorist but might be essential to an improvisor looking for an interesting accompaniment – were certainly common practice. There were many rules available to the player but with stylistic consistency as his main aim it is likely that his observation of them would be largely pragmatic.

From this information then the accompanist would fashion his part, deciding the general harmonic sound and density by his chord voicing. But the continuo was not to be just a succession of chords. Heinichen again: 'The art of the embellished thorough-bass, however, really consists of not always simply playing chords but of using an ornament here and there in all parts (particularly in the outermost part of the right hand, which usually stands out) and thereby giving more elegance to the accompaniment which can be applied with ease in four parts and, upon occasion, in five and six-part accompaniments.' Because he believes that embellishments depend less on rules than on practice and judgement and that they will, anyway, vary according to each performer's experience and taste, Heinichen is quite cautious and undogmatic in his advice. He divides embellishments into two groups, the first of which consists of those embellishments with a single, unchanging execution, a set device added to the accompaniment at the performer's discretion. He lists them as: the trill, transitus (passing notes), Vorschlag (appoggiatura), Schleiffung (slide), mordent and acciaccatura. He adds, 'ornaments are numberless', referring to the infinite variety of French Agréments and the (possibly even more prolific) Italian embellishments which were never, sensibly enough, fully codified or documented. These, Heinichen advises, 'we must leave to the visual

2 In the late and post baroque period a formalised, theoretical framework of rules was gradually imposed on the music. This, a mortal danger to any improvised music, manifested itself partly in a flood of textbooks on decoration. Commenting on these, Ferand writes: '... [they] point to a certain waning of the impulse to improvise – a truly creative art of ornamentation stimulated by the inspiration of the moment is replaced by the rationalistic mechanising trend towards the convenient employment of diminution formulas supplied "ready made" ' There is an unmistakable parallel between the situation described by Ferand and the condition of jazz in recent years where, as development comes to a standstill and the role for invention diminishes, the number of college courses, summer schools and text books devoted to it grows.

demonstration of a teacher or to the individual industry and experience of the student'. Heinichen's second group of embellishments include melody, passaggi (scalar patterns), arpeggios and imitation. These are all standard devices used in any harmony-based improvisation but in current baroque practice the arpeggio would appear to overshadow all the other embellishments of this second group and in its most common form is a full-voiced chord broken from the lowest note of the left hand to the highest of the right. Or again, quite commonly, a simple arpeggio in the left hand combining with an unbroken chord in the right hand. There is no evidence that much attention is now paid to Heinichen's advice to 'seek to learn from fine performers the many other ways of breaking chords'. The other ornaments in Heinichen's second list seem hardly to have survived at all. Certainly, melody improvisation, or the improvisation of a separate part, is rarely found now and if attempted is likely to be heavily disapproved of. A nice example of the change in attitude towards this practice is found in Mr.J.Westrup's *Musical Interpretation* published in 1971. He tells how J.S.Bach 'would, on occasion, accompany a trio in such a way that by adding a new melodic part he converted it into a quartet', then, realising the seditiousness of such an idea, adds, 'there is no need to suppose that we should take this as a criterion for accompanying Bach's own music or any other music of the same period'.

Melody improvisation, or the improvisation of a completely separate part, in accompaniment as opposed to solo playing, was always somewhat controversial. But that it was widely practised seems to be undeniable and is born out by the constant references to it by contemporary writers such as J.E.Daube, C.P.E.Bach, F.Gasparini, J.Matheson[3], and, of course, Heinichen, all of whom while bemoaning its prevalence, offer instruction in it and certainly don't suggest that it should be abolished. Post-baroque period authorities (including F.T.Arnold, whose *The Art of Accompaniment from a Thorough-Bass* (1931) is considered the most exhaustive account of thorough-bass playing) treat melody improvisation as an unnecessary evil. But it is plain that the theoretician has always seen it as part of his duty to keep a stern eye on the activities of the executant[4] and, as far as possible, limit the damage he can do. As Mr Westrup says: 'The enjoyment of performers can hardly be accepted as an aesthetic criterion.'

And so we arrive at the 20th century view of things. But before turning to the current practice of baroque I would like to take a final quotation from

3 In addition to his *Kleine General-Bass Schule* (1735), which offers comprehensive instruction in the art of accompanying from the first rudiments to the most complex figures, J.Matheson wrote two books on the art of extemporising solo pieces from given basses.

4 Hermann Finck, writing about 4-part vocal improvisation in 1556, warns his readers that 'No doubt a sharp-eyed one can be found who will search anxiously through everything and dissect it alive to see if he can detect anything... to which he feels he must object.'

J.D.Heinichen. Discussing the prevalence of controversy and argument, particularly between young and old in his time, he writes: 'The old musicians side more with reason, but the new with the Ear; and since both parties do not agree on the first fundamental, it is evident that the conclusions and consequences made from two contrary fundamental principles should breed just as many controversies of inferior rank and thousands of diametrically opposed hypotheses. Musicians of the past, we know, chose two judges in music: Reason and the Ear. The choice would be correct since both are indispensable to music; yet, because of the use of these two concomitants, the present cannot reconcile itself with the past, and in this the past is guilty of two errors. First, it wrongly classed the two judges and placed the Ear, the sovereign of music, below the rank of Reason or would divide its commanding authority with the latter. Whereupon the blameless Ear must immediately cede half of its monarchical domain. In addition, unfortunately, the composers of the past poorly explained the word *ratio*. In those innocent times (in which one knew nothing of present-day good taste and brilliance in music, and every simple harmony seemed beautiful) they thought Reason could be put to no better use than the creation of supposedly learned and speculative artificialities of note writing... Thus, one no longer had cause to ask if the music sounded well or pleased the listener, but rather if it looked good on paper. In this way, the Visual imperceptibly gained the most in music and used the authority of the imprudent Reason only to cover its own lust for power. Consequently, the suppressed Ear was tyrannized so long until finally it hid behind tables and chairs to await from the distance the condescending, merciful glance of its *unsurpatores regni (ratio & visus)*... It is...absurd if one should say along with pedants: this is outstanding music because it looks so fine (I mean pedantic) on paper, even though it does not please the ear, for which music is surely made... As we must now admit unanimously that our *Finis musices* is to stir the affects and to delight the ear, the true *Objectum musices*, it follows that we must adapt all our musical rules to the Ear.'

BAROQUE

(2)

That the present revival of baroque should produce a music which is completely different in character from the original is, perhaps, inevitable. The aims and philosophy of a revival are hardly those of an exploration. William J.Mitchell, in the introduction to his 1949 translation of C.P.E.Bach's *Versuch über die wahre Art das Clavier zu spielen*, complains: 'The extemporaneous realisation of a figured bass is a dead art. We have left behind us the period of the basso continuo and with it all the unwritten law, the axioms, the things that were taken for granted: in a word, the spirit of the time.' Lionel Salter in explanation:

Well, this is partly because of the conditions of the present day. We've all become so conditioned by modern recording techniques and by broadcasting...everybody's afraid to put a foot wrong. You see, these days, if you're going to have a record which is going to be played many times then a simple thing which didn't fit terribly well on one occasion wouldn't matter, but on repeated hearings it's going to jar like anything. So, we are all inhibited by recording into playing something which is set and perfect and therefore the element of chance – and after all there is always the chance that things won't come off – has been neglected. And this is totally at variance with the whole spirit of the baroque.

I'm not at all sure that recording is useful for anything more than reference. You have to react to the conditions of performance – the actual circumstances. You play differently in a different hall. The acoustics make a difference. The instrument makes a tremendous difference. You may be feeling more – I don't know – you may be feeling more worked up on this occasion – you feel something brighter is needed. You go into the music in a kind of – unbuttoned way, and if you play something which doesn't fit absolutely perfectly, well, it doesn't matter too much. You've really got to be on your toes, to be alert to do something which occurs to you which may seem a good idea, and be prepared also to find that it doesn't absolutely work. But it wouldn't matter because then the thing is alive, it's got some vitality in it.

A serious regression, in the current practice of baroque has been the appearance of 'authorised versions' for the continuo part. In many cases now the performer is presented with a fully written out accompaniment to play. Did Lionel Salter come across this situation?

Oh yes, in some cases they are very good, and, if you haven't the skill in improvisation, then by all means use them. But, more probably, I think the thing is to use this as a guide, as a basis, until you have got to the stage of being able to improvise your own part. What is necessary is that you have a real understanding, first of all, of harmony – keyboard harmony. That is the most important thing of all. Then a sense of style, then a rapport with whoever you are playing with. Then you will find yourself imitating lines and making counterpoints against them. You haven't really a model, you know. You can read all the various authorities on the subject, some more detailed than others, but the only thing which is common to them all is that they contradict one another madly. So at the end of it all you are not really very clear as to what was done. But you have to learn – for example – to differentiate between French and Italian style. You have to differentiate among various periods, and very often these days, with the great popularity of the harpsichord, you get a great many people who sit down at the instrument and proceed to show off their skill at continuo, and one hears something which is totally out of keeping with the genuine style of the music. So that you need, in fact, a fairly strict knowledge of the period, and then, within that, you need the freedom to do what you think is fit. But you still get conductors, you know, who don't understand what a continuo part should be and who are unprepared to let the performer do anything at all.

There are many things you can do. You can take the melodic outline of the violin part and imitate it. Sometimes you think that particular phrase will be useful, sometimes you pick on another one. It just depends on what you think at that moment. But it's something which has to be spontaneous. This is the essential part of it.

In recent years, authenticity in the performance of baroque music has become a barnyard of debate, at times deeply acrimonious. All kinds of intriguing notions about the performance, even the purpose, of music have been raised. Understandably, improvisation is rarely, if ever, mentioned in these wrangles. If the object of the activity is to reproduce as exactly as possible some agreed, authenticated example of the music of an earlier time, improvisation clearly becomes a problem. The one ineradicable difference between then and now must be the performer's attitude towards style, his way of performing the music, in effect *his* authenticity. However assiduously practised, the adoption of an earlier, preserved, and undevelopable style can, in improvisation, only be an inhibition unknown to the player of the former time. He, being the embodiment of the style – being the source of the style – couldn't have that type of problem. While he would be aware of the regional and national differences, performing baroque music would be for him his natural way of

27

playing. And not the least part of this would be his assumption that improvisation was an automatically accepted part of performing music. What is quite certain is that his main concern was *not* the preservation, in as unchanged a state as possible, of a 250- year-old music.

* * *

One of the strengths, one of the unique qualities of improvisation, is that it can, on occasion, transform a performance into something much better, much higher, than expected. Whether through the performance of an individual or of a group, and regardless of material, the music can be elevated by an unexpected development produced by the improvisation. I tried to discover from Lionel Salter whether this sort of thing was possible in the present day performance of baroque. Could the performance ever be remarkable because of a performer's contribution rather than for the composer's music? His reply reflected, I think, the general view held in this music.

That would be an absolute artistic crime.

So, whatever the position in earlier times, it seems that improvisation, when found, now has a strictly defined, controlled role in baroque. A role which is confined to complementing the fixed, documented part of the tradition. In effect, in order to preserve what is now the unchanging face of baroque, improvisation has been deprived of its usual function of being the sap through which music renews and reinvigorates itself and, if used at all, is retained to serve only as a carefully controlled decorative device.

ORGAN

(1)

'From writings of the Church fathers and other reports, it is unequivocally clear that the rites of worship of the early Christians were marked by a religious ecstasy that manifested itself in unhampered, purely emotional, spontaneous expression.' From the earliest time onward there is copious documentary evidence of the extensive part played by improvisation throughout the development of all church music. In vocal music improvising on all the intervals and internal combinations appearing in Gregorian chant was systematically practised by singers and choirboys. Later, instrumentally, there is evidence that musicians such as the 14th-century blind organist Francesco Landini became well-known for their improvising abilities.

The ways in which the drive to improvise manifested itself amongst the early organists and harpsichordists was most clearly observed as:

1) Embellishment (coloration, diminution) of a vocal or instrumental melody either borrowed or newly invented. (There are instruction manuals in this particular art dating from the 16th century).

2) The polyphonic treatment of a liturgical or secular *cantus firmus* by adding contrapuntal voices, as well as the spinning out of given or newly invented motifs in imitative style.

3) Free improvisation employing the possibilities inherent in the instrument for chord playing and passage work which led to the first autonomous forms of purely instrumental music – preambles, preludes, toccatas and fantasias.

Throughout the 17th and 18th centuries improvisation continued to play a major part in the development of church organ music, so much so that a comprehensive historical account of improvisation at this time would need a number of books (and authors) of its own. Even in the mid and late 19th century, which otherwise seems to have been a depressing time for European improvisation, there continued to be many organists who were known as improvising virtuosi.[1] In the 20th century the main development seems to have been concert improvisation which has become, particularly in France, a specialised and highly developed activity.

---

1 S.S.Wesley, 1810–1876, was reputed to have anticipated later harmonic developments in his playing, which is not a surprising phenomenon to anyone familiar with the possibilities of improvisation.

The main reason for the survival and continuous development of improvisation in organ playing, when throughout the rest of European classical music improvisation was being neglected or suppressed, is probably the adaptability and purely practical inventiveness required of any church organist in his working situation, a situation in which the creation of music is a necessity. For, although there is an enormous repertoire of music for use in any form of church service, it is normal practice for the organist to 'provide' music in many parts of a service. Voluntaries, interludes and postludes are often improvised. Even in playing written music, the tradition of Pavlovian exactitude found in orchestral playing is absent and the performer is 'allowed' considerable freedom. But also the instrument, the organ, in all its many forms and developments, has probably played a part in encouraging improvisation in this field. Even now, and in former times the position was much more extreme, there is no such thing as a typical organ. Every instrument is likely to contain so many individual characteristics that the first use of it will probably be in some measure exploratory. Then there is the somewhat indeterminate general character of the organ: the lack of a single accepted instrumental sound, the imprecise nature of even the best actions, the infinite variations of tone made possible by chorus and stop combinations; all these features give it a peculiar appropriateness for improvisation. Faced with such an enormous variety of instrumental possibilities, choice becomes an essential part of any performance.

Whatever the reasons for it, extemporisation, which seems to be the preferred word here, is now a completely accepted and integrated part of the organist's musicianship. It has, in fact, received the 'straight' world's ultimate acceptance and become a formal academic study. What effect this has had on the practice of improvisation is difficult to say, but it might account for the fact that this seems to be the only area in which musicians speak about – or even write about – their improvising in a technical way, although the organists with whom I discussed improvisation were in no way confined only to that approach.

Organ improvisation exists mainly in two clearly defined areas: strict – improvisation within set forms (composition forms); and free – which is simply improvisation not within set forms. The former is usually found in a concert situation and free improvisation is usually employed as it is required by the church organist. One is the formal presentation of improvisation, the other is its practical application in the church. Strict improvisation is the area with which the academic world is mainly concerned and it is also the subject of much of the very extensive literature on organ improvising.

Improvisation á l'Orgue, published in 1925 and generally considered as the definitive work on improvisation, was written by the French organist, improvisor and composer Marcel Dupré (1886–1971). A student of the improvisor and teacher Alexandre Guilmant (pupils of Dupré's having a close interest in improvisation included Joseph Bonnet, Louis Vierne, Olivier Messian, Jean Langlais and Nadia Boulanger), Dupré for many years always concluded his recitals with an improvisation and it is believed that a number of his compositions are transcriptions of his improvisations.

Dupré makes it clear that he is offering no simple task. 'Pour être bon improvisateur il faut non seulement avoir acquis une technique souple et súre, mais encore savoir l'Harmonie, le Contrepoint, la Fugue, et n'ignorer ni le Plein-Chant, ni le Composition, ni l'Orchestration.' He then sub-divides his book in the following way:

Chapter 1: Organ technique.

Chapter 2: Harmony.

Chapter 3: The Theme, includes a section on oriental and occidental modes – rhythm – analysis of theme.

Chapter 4: Counterpoint, a number of exercises and analyses of movements in different forms and Chorale (4 forms), examples from Catholic hymns and from J.S.Bach.

Chapter 5: Suite, describes and gives examples.

Chapter 6: Fugue, analyses subject and gives description of plan. Gives many examples of subjects used in Paris Conservatoire examinations between 1897–1923.

Chapter 7: Variations, description of different types and styles found in composition.

Chapter 8: Symphonic form, description of construction and examples.

These chapters describing set form constitute 95% of the book and deal with compositional technique, general musicianship, explain the framework within which improvisation must work and give some account of materials which can be used. Any element which is essentially to do with improvisation does not appear. There is one remaining, very brief, chapter on free improvisation (formes libres) and an appendix which discusses where improvisation is used in the different Catholic Offices.

A clearer indication of the nature of improvisation might sometimes be found in discussions of what is referred to as 'free' improvisation. This is usually mixed in somewhere with the generalised advice, the 'practical hints' section, which is often a feature of organ instruction books. In fact there is a corner of organ literature which is exclusively devoted to offering this sort of advice. These books, containing tips and practical hints, seem very often to date from the period 1910–1940 and are usually written by a working church organist for the edification and assistance of his peers and they often contain really useful advice for any kind of improvisor. Concerned exclusively with practical matters, problems organists might meet in their working situation, they contain the fruits of a great deal of improvising experience. In books such as *Playing the Organ, The Country Organist and Choirmaster, Church Organ Accompaniment, Organ Playing* and *The Complete Organist,* it is usually possible to find something useful about the practical aspects of improvising. And there are books wholly concerned with that side of the subject – H.Schouten in his *Improvisation on the Organ,* referring to the formal settings for improvisation which are normally studied, says: 'This, however, is not the last word about improvisation, for all church organists are confronted by improvisation problems Sunday after Sunday. The average church organist does not need to improvise fugues and passacaglias, rondos and scherzos... Every church organist, however, must be able to elaborate on a musical phrase taken from the liturgy in a simple, cohesive and responsible way.' (Schouten's book is actually very thorough and is divided into sections which cover harmonic improvisation, polyphonic improvisation and improvising polyphonic chorale preludes. He modestly stresses that his book should be regarded purely as an introduction to the art of improvisation, something which is worth emphasising about any book on the subject.)

Not quite in the category of the pocket-sized hints book is *The Art of Improvisation* by T.Carl Whitmer, published in 1934. This is more comprehensive, with quite an extensive technical section. But what is most remarkable about this book is its lack of defensiveness. Unusually for this area, Whitmer doesn't find it necessary to apologise for improvisation and looks upon it not only as a necessary expedient but also as a preferred activity. And there is no mention at all of 'instant composition'. However, he does take the student through all the usual manipulative devices, but his method is very compact and, usefully, he employs the same two bar phrase for every treatment throughout the book. This idea, of practising improvisation on a single limited idea, is often very effective.

Whitmer says: 'In general there are two ways to improvise. The first is by expansion and the other is by use of a set form.' On improvising on a set form, he says: 'It is not necessary to remember all details but it is necessary to recall plan and method and general character. Whenever in doubt use some set form, but experiment with expansion until you get this one thought deep down, "In expansion the form is generated. It makes itself".'

The following are a few typically vigorous pieces of advice from Whitmer's 'General Basic Principles':

'Don't look forward to a finished and complete entity. The idea must always be kept in a state of flux.'

'An error may be only an unintentional rightness.'

'Do not get too fussy about how every part of the thing sounds. Go ahead. All processes are at first awkward and clumsy and "funny".'

'Polishing is not at all the important thing; instead strive for a rough go-ahead energy.'

'Do not be afraid of being wrong; just be afraid of being uninteresting.'

He also has something to say about the usefulness of sheer imitation – following a model – and also its dangers. 'When it comes to the point of the pupil apeing his teacher the adult is in greater peril than the child. Children are naturally insurgent and when they have once acquired a measure of assurance they will fight for their own ideas as few adults care to do.'

Whitmer's enthusiasm for the uniqueness and special musical character of improvisation is, however, fairly untypical. It is much more common to find improvisation recommended only as a useful adjunct to the organist's musicianship. As regards its musical worth, the usual view is that it can, at its highest, be compared to composition.[2]

* * *

Stephen Hicks, through his studies with Nadia Boulanger and with André Marchal, has close connections with the French school of organ improvisation. Presently organist of Weybridge Parish church, he is an authority on early French music and has undertaken a great deal of research into English ornamentation. I asked him about prizes for improvisation, something which is peculiar to the organ world.

Yes. In France a prize for improvisation is every bit as valuable as a prize for interpretation. The course at the conservatoire, I think, is based on improvisation. Interpretation is considered almost less important. Although I think it is a bad idea to think of interpretation and improvisation as different things because interpretation has to have an element of improvisation as well. Improvisation can be a great communicating link and if that link isn't there in the interpretation then I think you lose something.

What is the criteria for awarding prizes? What is looked for?

2 This view of improvisation as aspiring to be mistaken for composition is present throughout European classical music's relationship with improvisation. It is expressed by Weber after hearing Hummel improvise: 'He used, with masterly control, figures of all kinds in a supremely logical way in innumerable positions. One could not be more pure and exact in a notated work than he was on this occasion.' The catalogue of well-known improvisors in this music usually goes 'Bach, Beethoven, Vogler, Mozart, Paganini, Chopin, Liszt, Widor, Frank, etcetera' – all composers. A little closer to Whitmer's view is that of J.S.Petri who, writing in 1782, claims that the improvised fantasy is 'the highest degree of composition – where meditation and execution are directly bound up with one another'

Absolute control of technique. And I don't mean physical technique, I mean musical technique. If you like, the same sort of technique as you need for composition. And then after that, I think, imagination.

Are you asked to improvise in particular styles, particular periods?

Not normally. But you can do, of course. If there's a fugue you wouldn't normally do a fugue in a modern idiom. But, usually, there is a free improvisation as well which takes either the form of an improvised symphony – variations – sometimes they just say 'Prelude and fugue'.[3]

How would you define the difference between 'free' and 'strict' in organ improvisation?

Strict improvisation is normally on a theme and it's in a set pattern. Like the plain chant themes of earlier times. You either do a fugue, a canon, 4 or 5 part counterpoint – like the old masters. The style would depend on the material used. In practice, that is in services, this is not always suitable for modern improvisation. Free improvisation is left entirely to the player and should be modern or at least 20th Century in style. It does not necessarily have to be on a theme.

If you didn't choose a theme where would your material come from?

From imagination entirely.

What do *you* think makes a good improvisation?

My own reaction to improvisation is not only one of self-expression but of the necessity to fill a need in the course of the liturgy. It is important to be able to improvise in any style in order to be able to play suitably at every occasion. One cannot stress too much the importance of total mastery of the old disciplines of harmony, counterpoint, all types of canon and fugue. Too many improvisations fail because of a lack of polyphonic thinking in the player's musical and technical armour. This leads to an inability to cope with larger canvases even when they are largely harmonic in style.

I think liturgical improvisation depends entirely on atmosphere. That's the main point of improvising, to give an atmosphere at a particular time of service. To give a sense of communion with something, you see. Concert improvisation – I think that requires a certain showmanship, as well.

Concert improvisation for the organist is a somewhat specialist field. Here the musician demonstrates in public his ability to play extempore in all the basic composition forms and structures. He takes a theme – sometimes proposed by a member of the audience – and presents it in a succession of

---

3 Testing the skill of church organists in this way has a long history. The 'regolamento' in force even before 1540 at St.Mark's in Venice required the applicant first to play a fantasy on a given theme from a Kyrie or a motet in strict 4-part setting. After which he was expected to lead a cantus firmus from the choir-book fugally through all four parts and finally to imitate and answer in a modulation a verse from an unfamiliar composition sung by the chorus.

musical guises; – minuet, scherzo, march, waltz, rondo, sonata form, canon, fugue, basso ostinato, passacaglia. It seems to be common practice to have a certain amount of preparation before the performance – something to be found in all types of improvising, I think. Whitmer's advice on concert improvisation is: 'After all preparations are complete, go to it without any hesitancy, knowing that not more than one in the audience can do it any better.'

I asked Stephen Hicks if he thought in terms of success or failure in his improvisation.

Occasionally you play and you think – yes, that was quite good – but most of the time...I think an improvisation should be played and then forgotten.

It's appropriate or not and that's it?

It's either good or bad but if you listen to an improvisation over and over again it just gets worse. You hear more fifths, more octaves, more things you would never want to do again.

But it's of the nature of improvisation, I would have thought, that you don't listen to it over and over again. Without recording you couldn't, could you?

No, you couldn't, and I don't think you should. It's something that should be heard, enjoyed or otherwise, and then completely forgotten.

It may be that opponents and supporters of improvisation are defined by their attitude towards the fact that improvisation embraces, even celebrates, music's essentially ephemeral nature. For many of the people involved in it, one of the enduring attractions of improvisation is its momentary existence: the absence of a residual document.

ORGAN

In any discussion of present-day organ improvisation it quickly becomes apparent that the centre of that particular world is Paris. Stephen Hicks repeatedly referred to his studies there and to the many outstanding improvisors he had heard in Paris. Consequently I went there, listened to some of the music, and spoke to Jean Langlais, who was part of the Paris school of improvising organists for almost 50 years. A pupil of Marcel Dupré, he was the organist at St.Clothilde, the most recent of a long line of brilliant musicians to occupy that position, a succession which includes Charles Tournémire, Gilbert Pierné, and César Franck, all of them known as outstanding improvisors. I asked him about some of the earlier improvisors he had known, those who had established Paris as the centre for organ improvisation.

Widor was not a very fine improvisor. A great composer, a great organist, but I must confess his improvisation was very boring. There was Guilmant and there was Vierne. Vierne was a fantastic improvisor. And Tournémire. Tournémire was a really great improvisor. I heard him one day in St.Germain des Pres. He improvised for 45 minutes without any interruption and it was magnificent all the time. I also heard him once at Vespers where for the Magnificat he improvised alternate verses with the choir – the choir sang one verse – he improvised the second – the choir sang the third and Tournémire the fourth. The regular Magnificat is not too long, you know. If you sing everything it will last perhaps two minutes maximum but with Tournémire's improvisations it lasted twenty-four to twenty-five minutes.

In a long improvisation would it take place on a series of set forms or would it be free improvisation?

I don't think there is such a thing as free improvisation because for improvising it is necessary to know harmony, counterpoint and fugue plus improvisation. But Tournémire improvised everything; the form and the music, and that is very difficult. Dupré, for instance, improvised a lot of symphonies all over the world. And I too have played two hundred and seventy four recitals in the United States and in that time I did many symphonies, sonatas in five movements. But that is like an exercise one has practised for years. It is improvisation but using many things that one has practised for many years. The most important thing for an improvisor is to be able to think quickly. Fast.

It's common to find improvisation described as a type of instant composition, but are they not completely different types of activity producing completely different results?

Yes, an example of that is the difference between Tournémire's improvisation and his composition. And the same for Dupré. When Dupré composed he wrote music that was, I should say, modern. And when he improvised he was not so modern. He was a little bit classical. They were quite different. And you know, for me, right now, the greatest musician for the organ is Olivier Messiaen. He is a very good friend of mine for many years. We were together in Marcel Dupré's class and he did many things for me when I studied orchestration with Paul Dukas. Because I did not have the scores in Braille, Messiaen read the scores for me for many many years. If you are familiar with Messiaen's work and then go to the Trinité and listen to his improvisations you will not recognise him as the same musician. Very different. And sometimes, but this does not apply to Messiaen, sometimes the improvisor is more interesting than the composer.

Why has improvisation remained with organ playing even when in other parts of European classical music it more or less disappeared?

Because in churches we are obliged to improvise all the time. If a priest is very slow, we are obliged to adapt to that. If the priest is very fast we also have to adapt. We cannot play a Bach prelude, say. So we improvise everything. I don't think it is possible to be an organist if you are not also an improvisor. But people are also very interested in concert improvisation. Particularly the people who submit themes. I think composers are very interested to submit a theme and see what happens to it.

Because M.Langlais is blind I wondered exactly how he received a theme from a member of the audience.

I have two possibilities. The theme might be played by whoever submits it. Or someone dictates the theme and I write it down in Braille. And sometimes my son is with me and he plays the theme before I improvise. For example, I have played several times in the Royal Festival Hall in London and on one occasion a theme was submitted by Benjamin Britten. They gave the envelope containing the theme to my son, he opened the envelope and he played the theme, and then I started. That is really an improvisation. The theme was very good. It was in C minor, I remember.

I referred to a popular misconception about improvisation: that it is a totally instantaneous event completely lacking in forethought or preparation.

Earlier I mentioned that Messiaen studied in Marcel Dupré's class at the same time as I did. Well, the day he won the first prize in the competition he improvised a splendid fugue. But he practised two years for that. And he was

Messiaen. And we have only one Messiaen. We have a technique for practising improvisation like we have a technique for practising scales and arpeggios. The first thing you have to practise is to be able to reproduce on the organ what you are thinking. And any exercise for improvisation should allow less and less time for its performance so that the improvisor is obliged to think faster and faster. One exercise that is useful is to play a series of chords and improvise with each voice separately. But to improvise takes a very long time. Two weeks ago I was in Sweden and in between the concerts I gave classes. And I met a very gifted man, both for the organ and for improvisation. He was the winner of a competition in Haarlem. He said to me 'I would like to improvise something for you'. I gave him three themes. And he did something really free. I then realised that he was very gifted but that his background was not developed sufficiently. Then I said 'this is a very brief theme, do a trio with that'. And he was unable to do a trio. Well, now he has decided to come to Paris to study improvisation with me. He realised he was not informed about everything. And he was a prize winner. Improvisation can be very complicated. Those people who say 'I can improvise easily' – they are amateurs.

Do you think there are many different approaches to improvisation?

Of course, but I repeat, the most important thing for improvisation is to be able to think very quickly. And theoretically, a great improvisor must be able to improvise everything. Dupré said to us 'If you can improvise a trio, a classical trio, you are able to improvise a symphony'. And he was right.

Why do some musicians not improvise?

I don't know. Probably they are not interested or they do not have the background or they have no necessity for it. But modern composers say now 'I cannot say how long my work is. It depends on how long the orchestra improvises'. That is ridiculous.

Are you interested in any of the recent developments in composition which have to do with improvisation?

No. I accept everything if it is valuable or if it is a comparable progression within a system. But if you sit on the manuals – I don't agree.

Do you think there is any musical language that is more appropriate for improvisation than any other?

No, I don't think so. It depends on the improvisor. You know, that reminds me of a story. Vincent D'Indy was asked if he had any idea what the musical future was to be. D'Indy answered: 'The future will be what a genius decides it will be.' Improvisation is like that.

PART THREE

ROCK

Many rock instrumentalists and singers who have very little concern for the skills of instrumental improvisation nevertheless employ what could be called an improvising principle. Their material, although it might change very little, has to be at least flexible and capable of immediate adjustment. A performance is never entirely fixed and must be sensitive to unique performing factors. There is no abstract ideal, no scripted external yardstick, which stands above the performance and against which any performance has to be measured. Where anything is written down it serves not as a perfect expression of the music to be played but as a starting point, a guide. 'It doesn't matter who wrote it as long the right person is playing it.' However, as a clearly defined instrumental force which might affect the course of the music or in which a player might find his expression, improvisation wasn't much in evidence in rock until around 1967/68. I asked Steve Howe, the guitarist with the group Yes, who provided the above quote, about this.

Yeah, the '67 period of psychedelic music brought it all in. All the young guitarists and other musicians as well felt that they could play on these planes – play long improvised solos. I was doing it myself and so were a lot of other guitarists and keyboard players. For some reason that particular period, and the feeling that was going on between the people everyone was working with, was very much that one could have a song – and improvisation was really to expand the whole idea of what a song had been up to then in a single way. It all ties up with the expansion of the selling commodity – the change from the single to the album. As soon as there was some more space there was time to be more loose and to play. I think there were more people just trying to get out of the rut of playing a song that repeated its first strain and then its middle eight and then the first eight again, you know. I think a lot of things were understood better after that time. I felt like that, I let loose for about a year. You have to be very, very good to make it work. The music did widen out a lot at that time. Because there was the country influence coming back; jazz affected it, which is one of the most important aspects for me; and there was the Indian music thing. All of a sudden it seemed to be all there at once. It was becoming a much warmer thing where people could improvise much more freely.

The derivation of almost all improvisation in rock is the blues. The main model for a rock musician is usually to be found amongst the black American blues players. What little improvising there is outside of this influence is usually of an experimental nature deriving mainly from electronic music.

People have thought of the guitar for years in a blues vein and Hendrix did coordinate the blues and modern rock, you know, but in addition to that sort of thing and the experimental things there is a third role which I've wanted to fill most of all. I've always wanted to be a total middle guitarist in rock, doing the fundamental rock thing as well as forming some more modern clichés. But I don't think everybody fits into these categories. Once you come down to it there are many missing links between the actual and the labelling in any kind of music. Improvisation really moves when it's a top rate somebody who sets some kind of standard and has a style. And I think people search for this in their improvisation.

What makes one improvisation better than another?

Basically a certain feeling of clearness of thinking about what I am doing. Very often I can accept virtually any improvisation I do. I've done things at home, just improvised once and said 'That's fine'. Other times I've got involved in it and reached for something a bit more completely free of clichés in phrasing, you know. Not necessarily notes, but more in phrasing – I keep using the words accurate and exact – clarity of phrasing. This thing really excites me – that's what I will accept... It's got the notes well pushed out – each note having a value for itself. I think that's a thing people, most people, strive for. Some positiveness about it. I can meander endlessly and if I'm making a recording I think I know what I'm after. I'm after grasping something. There's a little bit more than I think I am capable of, you know, and if I can get it then I'm happy. I try and set a standard. In fact, I think this applies to groups; that there is a standard in improvisation which until you've reached that you can't possibly play well – not really united. Once you've really played well together on an improvised section I think that raises the whole standard of the tour.

You mentioned earlier how you improvise into a cassette recorder and listen back to it and how that was part of your composing method.

I do exactly that. What I usually try and do is mix the idea of writing music and improvising together, if you like. So, if I am working on any kind of music I might play that and then wander off into something – something else off the top of my head. And if I really like it I usually try and use it because I feel that if something came like that – well, I like things that come easy. Improvising does come reasonably easy. I virtually always improvised, even my earliest kind of work when I used to play in pubs, when I was 14 or 15, before I left school. I used to improvise in one way or another. I'd be interested now to hear what I played.

One of the things about improvising: it's very hard to judge it until after you've gone through a period of a few years. I tend to look back on things that I've played as things that used to do something to me and think 'Well, you had that a few years ago, but does it still get me off?' In the same way I try to watch my progress, judging it by the improvisation quite often.

Have you ever tried actually reproducing an improvisation of your own from a cassette made earlier? Something you like, so you try and run it off again?

I had to do it with an album. When we'd finished I rushed home and learnt two or three of the guitar breaks.

When you are playing them later what's the difference between the first time you played them and reproducing them?

It's never quite as magical. But then again it turns into a piece of music, a tune. It's now a melody. It changes from the idea of being an improvisation to playing a melody.

We discussed a section of the Yes album *Topography of the Oceans* which featured a guitar improvisation and I asked Steve Howe if he had recorded it in one take, or whether, in fact, he had recorded a series of improvisations and selected his preferred one for the record.

I think over a few days I had quite a few goes at it. Normally I do a few takes and have a listen to them and then, hopefully, I know the direction. I wanted a slightly melancholy beginning, building up to a lavish kind of finish, which is only ended by the group stating seven beats – it's our seventh album and lots of things happen in sevens, and that particular side starts with seven beats. I think the sensation I was trying to get was that the guitar was behind the group. It was trying to catch up with the group. The group kept moving to another chord and the guitarist is just reaching – yes! he got it. Then they climbed again and it climbed again. I used every fret on the guitar on this one, I think.

When you start to play off the top of your head, that's when the truth is really known about people. I think that is why there is a certain amount of caution in talking about it. Somebody said that if you try to look at inspiration too closely it disappears. Well, it's like that. Untangible.

* * *

Nothing reflects change more speedily than popular music, and the cultural climate in which the improvising rock instrumentalist flourished in the 1960s and '70s is pretty much extinct. By the 1990s, his skills are likely to have been superseded by the latest piece of technology. The fact that improvisation, irrepressible as ever, has seeped into many of the uses of that technology is probably not much compensation to the redundant instrumentalist.

Seemingly untouched by the vagaries of fashion and taste, however, is The Grateful Dead. For over a quarter of a century they have continued playing and while this is not unique, even in this area, they are the only rock band whose performances are based on the idea of improvisation and, unusual in any area, whose reputation is based on the expectation of change.

The following is drawn from conversations I had with Jerry Garcia in 1990. He is, for many people, *the* improvising rock guitar player. I asked him what he thought about discussing these things, the unsuitability of the language normally used in discussing music.

It's not an appropriate language because most people don't speak it and it only talks about proportions and so forth. It doesn't really say much about emotional content, for example, or character or any number of other things.

You've talked about chaos obscuring other kinds of organisation.

It's a matter of how many levels you can apprehend. I don't think there's really much limit to layers of visual information but with sound there are diminishing returns. It has to get up to where it's almost totally blanket noise before you can hear a lot. In The Grateful Dead when when we're playing very open with no structure, sometimes the sound level can speed a sensory overload of a kind which starts to become a physical experience rather than a musical one and that also has a certain kind of value. What's interesting to me is the accidental, the chaotic. You know, the stuff that you can't control or you can't predict.

There's another side to that isn't there, which it seems to me you're interested in. Magic...

This is part of the tradition of music, where music comes from. A magic of one sort or another. For us, for The Grateful Dead, that has been part of what's kept us going all this time. It's sort of stumbling into this area where there's a lot of energy and a lot of something happening and not a lot of control. So that the sense of individual control disappears and you are working at another another level entirely. Sometimes this feels to me as though you don't have to really think about what's happening. Things just flow. It's kind of hard to report on but it's a real thing. I mean we've checked it out with each other and after twenty-five years of exploring some of these outer limits of musical weirdness this is stuff that we pretty much understand intuitively but we don't have language to talk about it. But it's reported back to us by people in the audience too so this is one of those things where we're sort of collecting data without really knowing quite where it's leading or what it's about but we feel a certain custodian relationship to it. It's not something that we're creating exactly, in a way it's creating us. Musically speaking we're not really making decisions about it and we certainly don't discuss it. It's something that breaks out every now and again. We can't make it happen either. It defies analysis but it's certainly something to wonder about.

You've had this almost unique experience in that because of your neurological illness and your subsequent recovery you've had to learn to play the guitar twice and I wondered just what that meant from an improvisation point of view.

It was as though my whole experience as a player were some fragile crystal chandelier or something and somebody took a hammer and smashed it. Something like that. So there are fragments all over the place. The thing of re-learning the neuro pathways, regrouping the neuro pathways, so that 'this' means a finger moves, and 'that' means another finger moves, that whole biological language, was in there somewhere and a certain amount of it my muscles remembered, even if I didn't. So I could play say a B flat major seventh without knowing that that was what it was. Having the concept over here and the facility over there and bringing the two of them together, that's what it was like. I was aware of both sides but it was a matter of bringing them together seamlessly. In a way, it made it so that everything was fresh again. So all of a sudden the Blues was great you know and the simplest structures, the simplest tunes, it just made it all really great. It's like hearing everything with a fresh ear. I mean the nice thing about having Alzheimers Disease is that you only need to know one joke and it's funny every time you hear it. You forget what the punchline was. Music, everything, became fresh to me again and it enthuses your playing. So I think now I'm probably playing better than I used to play. That thing of having to shift in point of view, I think, is very valuable.

AUDIENCE

The relationship between any music which is improvised and its audience is of a very special nature. Improvisation's responsiveness to its environment puts the performance in a position to be directly influenced by the audience. Invoking professionalism – the ability to provide at least a standard performance whatever the circumstances – usually has a deleterious effect on improvisation, causing it to be confined to the more predictable aspects of idiom or vocabulary. Therefore, the effect of the audience's approval or disapproval is immediate and, because its effect is on the creator at the time of making the music, its influence is not only on the performance but also on the forming and choice of the stuff used. From the excesses of the improvised cadenza in the 19th century to the more bizarre parts of Norman Granz's Jazz at the Philharmonic in the 1950s, the dangers to an improvisor of audience 'appreciation' have been regularly demonstrated. Alain Danielou, writing about the difficulties for Asian musicians working within the Occidental entertainment system describes exactly the problem which has also affected Western performance musics such as flamenco, jazz and, increasingly, 'free' music. 'When the musicians note a positive reaction from the public, they are tempted to reproduce the effect which provoked this reaction and consequently one can understand how the rapid deterioration of the music performed could occur. The musician becomes little by little an actor who repeats his tricks when he notices that the public reacts favourably. His concerts change gradually into a music-hall number from which inspiration is excluded or is transformed into a commercial method.'

And yet, to improvise and not to be responsive to one's surroundings is a contradiction if not an impossibility. So a lot of questions can be asked about improvising before an audience and apparently answering them is not easy. Undeniably, the audience for improvisation, good or bad, active or passive, sympathetic or hostile, has a power that no other audience has. It can affect the creation of that which is being witnessed. And perhaps because of that possibility the audience for improvisation has a degree of intimacy with the music that is not achieved in any other situation.

Steve Howe: *I think the audience do contribute an awful lot, but I don't quite know how to talk about it because it can make me so excited. I've seen myself on film improvising and been surprised at what I happened to do –*

*wandering around – moving my face – not really conscious of that at the time.
And I start to see a connection between – once you start leading a piece of
music you do start walking out towards the audience. You start kind of
directing yourself at the audience. Well, you get this kind of call, almost.*

The improvisation you make at home must be very different to the
improvisation you do in public?

Steve Howe: *That's possibly a thing I've thought about most – I consider
what I play at home as being quite unique against what I do on stage. I think
when the audience is there there's a demand for it to be good, and when you're
at home, because there's no demand, it's so laid back that I think you can come
up with some of your best music...when there is no call.*

Ronnie Scott, who gives his views on improvisation in jazz in the next
chapter, had something to say about audiences.

*You can't divorce playing this kind of music from the fact that there is an
audience, you can't play it in a vacuum. It's got to be something that
communicates otherwise it doesn't mean very much. I mean, you could sit in
your front room and think you are playing fantastically and if there's no
audience it doesn't mean anything.*

And yet you could think you were playing fantastically?

Ronnie Scott: *Well – you'd think 'My God, my technique is good today
and I couldn't play that last night' – something like that – but then go out in
front of an audience and play – it's a different thing, I find.*

Later in the conversation: I'd just like to go back to one thing: you
wouldn't feel that it would be possible to get a peak performance, if I can put it
that way, without an audience?

Ronnie Scott: *There must be someone there, because I can't think that it
means very much if you're playing to nobody, I mean even if it's other
musicians in the group you're playing with.*

It's nothing to do with the size of an audience, then?

*Oh no, I don't think so but it's some kind of communication on that level
which is peculiar to music...*

The views of Ronnie Scott and Steve Howe on this subject contrasted
quite sharply with those expressed by Viram Jasani and Paco Peña.

Viram Jasani: *I personally feel that with a lot of Indian musicians it's
actually at the time that they practice that their best creative powers come out,
because they are really free – they're not worried about an audience sitting
there and this is a time when they really let themselves go – a musician
obviously will try to put on his best performance before an audience, but he
feels restricted. He's very careful.*

45

Paco Peña had this to say: *The audience for flamenco has never been as wide as it is now and really, it doesn't seem natural.*

What doesn't seem natural?

Paco Peña: *If you have a large audience, you know, it's somehow — somehow it doesn't seem to give it a chance to be what it really is. Playing before an audience is always a compromise.*

Among improvisors, Jerry Garcia has a unique relationship with his audience. Not only is it huge but for The Grateful Dead there are thousands of people who, sometimes over a period of years, attend their concerts regularly in order to enjoy the changes in the music. Deadheads, as their fans call themselves, attend successive concerts and compare – in a magazine published largely for this purpose – reports of the band's performances, reports which highlight and discuss the changes and differences between one performance and another.

I put it to Jerry Garcia: You have a very special audience in that many of them come to see you over and over again and they don't come to hear what they've heard before.

Absolutely not.

So perhaps you've got a kind of ideal improvisor's audience?

Well, I think that you have to train the audience, that's all. I think if you say – what we're doing here is we're inventing this as we go along and you too are involved in this experience and it's never going to be this way again, this is it for this particular version – then there's value to that and I think an audience, our audience, is the proof of that. These are people who will come back to every performance. If we do ten days somewhere a lot of them will be back every night and they know that it's gonna be different every night. Another interesting thing: my perception of what's a good night for us may be totally different from everybody else's perception. The audience has a great night listening to us struggle, feeling that we never quite get together. Sometimes we struggle the whole night without ever feeling like we've agreed on anything and sometimes the audience loves that. You know for them sometimes that's the best stuff. So again the reporting is difficult. They're very involved and they feel in fact as responsible in some ways as we do. They share the responsibility for the music, which I think is appropriate. I mean they're there and they're culpable you know. If not guilty then certainly culpable.

What's the difference when you are playing on your own, when the group plays without an audience?

...I think we're more adventurous publicly. I think we go for it more before an audience because that's been our structure, that's our place, you know. The audience expects us to do it, we're comfortable doing it, and so we

tend to be more experimental, I think. We don't do our best playing privately, which is backwards from a lot of musicians. The audience has gotten to be a homebase for us which allows the freedom to explore, I think.

* * *

So you can take your pick out of these opinions. Ernst Fischer wrote: 'It is essential to distinguish between music the sole purpose of which is to produce a uniform and deliberate effect, thus stimulating a collective action of an intended kind, and music whose meaning is, in itself, expressing feelings, ideas, sensations, or experiences, and which, far from welding people into a homogeneous mass with identical reactions, allows free play to individual subjective associations.'

Which might explain everything; but this is now a pretty unfashionable view. The conventional wisdom now allows only one audience and it knows no limits, it is omniscient and it is to be courted by everyone. To play in a manner which excludes the larger audience or, worse, *to prefer* to play before a small audience, is taken as an indication that the music is pretentious, elitist, 'uncommunicative', self-absorbed and probably many other disgusting things too. So what can an improvisor say about audiences? The propaganda of the entertainment industry and the strenuous, if futile, efforts of the art world to compete with it, combine to turn the audience into a body of mystical omnipotence. And what it seems to demand above all else is lip-service.

Incidentally, the solution offered by the jazz musician Charlie Parker to the problem of improvising in front of an audience was to turn his back on it, a position favoured by the church organist. A bit extreme, perhaps, but musically speaking, it's doubtful if Parker would have done any better prostrating himself before it.

JAZZ

(1)

There is no doubt that the single most important contribution to the revitalisation of improvisation in Western music in the 20th century is jazz. A unique music with, in its earlier years, boundless vitality, the enormous musical and sociological importance, the world-wide influence, of jazz is now largely recognised. But for the Western musician its greatest service was to revive something almost extinct in Occidental music: it reminded him that performing music and creating music are not necessarily separate activities and that, at its best, instrumental improvisation can achieve the highest levels of musical expression.

It was probably during the 1950s that jazz first gave signs of running out of steam. By the 1960s it had moved into a series of changes which led Rex Stewart in 1965 to prophesy: 'In the foreseeable future most of the vitality and beauty of this U.S. art form will be found only in other countries in an adulterated form.' The results of these changes, such as free jazz and a sequence of hyphenated hybrids the most pervasive of which is jazz-rock, are not considered here. This chapter is concerned with improvisation in 'conventional' jazz. During the jazz revival of the late-1980s, this kind of playing – essentially formed in the 1940s and '50s – came to be accepted as the standard way of playing jazz. Perhaps a recognition that the various developments of the '60s and '70s were 'adulterated forms' which, in jazz terms, lead nowhere and left no alternative but to go back to the last period which manifested 'vitality and beauty' and to stick with that.

The easiest way to distinguish between conventional jazz and its offshoots is to describe the improvisation in conventional jazz as being based on tunes in time. The simple mechanics are that the improvisation is derived from the melody, scales and arpeggios associated with a harmonic sequence of a set length played in regular time. This vehicle is invariably one of the usual popular song forms or the blues (of the strict 12 bar kind). As the essentials of improvisation have very little to do with mechanics this type of description, as usual, gives absolutely no idea of how infinitely sophisticated this process can be. Some indication of the resourcefulness of this device, if it can be so described, is that one tune worked in this way might serve an improvisor as a productive vehicle for years. The repertoire of a jazzman such as Dexter Gordon or Lee Konitz, for instance, contains probably a fairly small number of different 'songs'. But they will provide an adequate working context, perhaps for a lifetime. Within these boundaries there is a continuous process of renewal in which old material is re-shaped and adjusted, sometimes rejected, and new material introduced. 'If I do an hour show, if I'm extremely fertile, there will be about fifteen minutes of pure ad-lib. But on an average it's about four or five minutes. But the fact that I've created it in ad-lib seems to give it a complete feeling of free form.'

This quote doesn't come from a musician, but from a comedian. Lenny Bruce often compared his working methods to those of the jazzman and here he emphasizes the importance of the introduction of new material. It doesn't only supply fresh stuff to work on, it imbues the whole with a spirit of freedom. (Paco Peña describes this phenomenon on page 16) It ejects what is no longer useful and revitalises the remaining material. Although the main concern is almost always for the maintenance of the identity and quality of the idiom it is the introduction of some, however little, new material which ensures the health and guarantees the survival of the whole.

* * *

For years the health of jazz has been a source of seemingly endless debate. While enthusiasts chant their support from the sidelines, the music itself now seems capable only of looking backwards. Each successive revival sees a further mining of its history and a music once rightly described as 'the sound of surprise' is now chiefly enjoyed as a reminder of yesteryear. The few surviving originators, musicians once justly renowned for their adventurousness and musical vision, are now celebrated in an endless round of festivals and anniversaries as the guardians of a tradition. Meanwhile, much of the music is represented by a host of younger players who have also, it seems, taken on the curatorship of 'their' tradition. This takes the form of uncannily accurate reproductions of the playing styles of an earlier period, archaisms sometimes reinforced by period dress and manner.

The reason usually offered as to why during the 1980s so many young players should have wanted to play so much old music – part of a politically reactionary time, with matching fashions – sounds convincing enough but at least a contributory cause might be that the mechanics of this particular style – its somewhat stylistic rigidity, its susceptiblity to formulated method – created a field day for the educators. Taking the music made by, say, Jack Teagarden or by Albert Ayler and extracting from it a 'method' is difficult to imagine. On the other hand, be-bop has obviously been the pedagogue's delight. It has proved to be one style of improvising which can be easily taught. And taught it is; in

49

colleges, music schools, night classes, prisons; through a constant flow of tutors, methods and 'how to' books, resulting in perhaps the first standardised, non-personal approach to teaching improvisation. The mechanics of the style are everywhere; of the restlessness, the adventurousness, the thirst for change which was a central characteristic of the jazz of that period there seems to be no sign at all.

There is a strange parallel between the course of jazz history and the career of Louis Armstrong, perhaps its greatest exponent. This is a contemporary account of his early playing: 'Louis Armstrong would improvise on the same theme for a full half-hour, taking twenty choruses in a row... His imagination seemed inexhaustible; for each new chorus he had new ideas more beautiful than those he had reproduced for the preceding chorus. As he went on, his improvisations grew hotter, his style became more and more simple – until at the end there was nothing but the endless repetition of one fragment of melody – or even a single note insistently sounded and executed with cataclysmic intonations' (H.Panassie in *Hot Jazz*). Whatever else might be said about it, that description is obviously about a quite different sort of musical experience from the totally formalised, ritual performances of old favourites with which Louis Armstrong in his later years never failed to transport his admirers. And it is possible to recognise a corresponding change in jazz as a whole. With Louis Armstrong, of course, the usual erosions of time, the wear and tear of a lifetime spent as a travelling musician and the exigencies of show business on a man who combined, perhaps uniquely, being a supreme creative artist with being one of the century's outstanding entertainers, are reasons enough for the change. Whether similar reasons can also account for some of the enfeeblement which has taken place in jazz, is at least a possibility. In any event, jazz, whatever the reasons, seems to have changed from an aggressive, independent, vital, *searching* music to being a comfortable reminder of the good old days.

* * *

Although its influence has been worldwide, from a playing point of view jazz has been unshakeably American. Europe, for instance, although virtually colonised by it, has still produced only Django Reinhardt as a possible exception to the rule that all great jazz musicians are American. (Of course, there is also the proposition that all the really significant figures in jazz are black. As these 'greats' seem to be recruited exclusively from that tiny proportion of the world's black population which is also American, that reinforces the point.)

In Britain, jazz has been played since the 1920s but, apart from a scattering of individuals, the local audiences' preference has always been, naturally enough, for the American variety. So, deprived, by definition, of the opportunity to compete artistically on equal terms and reduced by limited employment opportunities to the status of a side-line, British jazz, even at the best of times, has never shown any aspirations to be anything other than a deferential second best. Miraculously, in spite of this crippling musical environment, Britain has managed to produce a handful of very fine players. Players who in addition to being good jazz players have succeeded in the difficult task of maintaining a permanently wholehearted commitment to jazz while working as musicians in Britain.

Ronnie Scott is one of these. As far as I know he might agree with very little or none at all of the above but I chose to speak to him about improvisation in conventional jazz because, over many years, he has shown how it is possible, even for a non-American, to play within the central tradition of jazz and keep some independence of attitude and style. He has also, as the owner of one of the world's best known jazz clubs, been in a unique position to hear at the closest possible range all the greatest jazzmen of the past thirty years. But it was his own improvisation about which I asked him to talk.

When I started to play I didn't know really that there was such a thing as improvising. I used to think that the thing was to play the saxophone in a dance band. The realisation of improvisation grew with learning to play the instrument and then listening to records of jazz soloists and associating with other musicians of my own age who were trying to improvise. I think it grows from there and I think it's never ending, well, at least, I hope it is.

I feel that my own ability to improvise, such as it is, arises from a combination of experience – one learns what one can play and what one can't play – and that conjunction of sounds which is pleasing to one's ear, because I don't have a great harmonic knowledge, by any means. But I'm also convinced that there are as many attitudes and conceptions of, and manners of, improvisation, and ways of working towards improvisation, as there are people. Oscar Peterson for instance, is a very, very polished, technically immaculate, performer who – I hope he wouldn't mind me saying so – trots out these fantastic things that he has perfected and it really is a remarkable performance. Whereas Sonny Rollins, he could go on one night and maybe it's disappointing, and another night he'll just take your breath away by his kind of imagination and so forth. And it would be different every night with Rollins.

We got into the question of judging the quality of an improvisation.

I find there is a difficulty for me – I mean you can practice for hours, I've never really done it, but I've done what for me is a great deal of practice over a period of two or three weeks, and then played in public, and my technique feels worse than ever before, whereas, by the same token one can not touch the instrument for a few weeks and go out and be free and loose with the instrument, so, as far as the original question is concerned, how do I judge whether what I've played is...satisfactory, it is very difficult because what seems to happen is that one becomes unconscious of playing, you know, it becomes as if something else has taken over and you're just an intermediary between whatever else and the instrument, and everything you try seems to come off, or at least, even if it doesn't come off it doesn't seem to matter very much, it's still a certain kind of feeling that you're aiming for – or unconsciously aiming for – and when this happens – inspiration – duende – whatever you like to call it – a happy conjunction of conditions and events and middle attitudes – it will feel good. It will feel that 'I should be what I am' kind of thing.

I think you are conditioned by the instrument you play, also by the influences that other players before you or your contemporaries have had. There is a certain kind of feeling one gets when one finds oneself influenced by great players. There can be a danger when you're playing that, if it doesn't sound like one of the great players then it's not valid. This is something that I find myself, as I get older, growing farther and farther away from, you know, which I think is a good thing. One becomes much happier to sound like oneself rather than sounding like one of the recognised great tenor saxophone players. But there was a time when, if I didn't sound like whoever was the main man, then I didn't feel happy about it.

I would like ideally to be able to express my – I don't know – personality or whatever – musically, to the limits of my ability. I think that's all anybody can aim for, and I don't feel that I personally am the kind of musician that is going to come out with some fantastic innovation of any kind, but what I'm happy to do is to try and play in such a way that it would be recognisable as me, and it would express something to people about the way I feel about things. As I say, there are so many, almost limitless, attitudes towards improvisation dependent on one's talent and one's capabilities.

* * *

Jazz provides a good example of the dangers of sequacity in a largely improvised music. R.Strinavasan speaks of the same problem in Indian music: 'The enemy is mere imitation without imbibing the inspiration which makes the art a living thing.' The tendency to derivativeness and the prevalence of imitative playing in all idiomatic improvisation seems to have produced in jazz a situation where increasingly the music became identified with the playing style of a handful of musicians. Strangely enough, the number of acceptable models appears to get smaller as time goes on. The performing style of the rest, the vast majority of players, is invariably identified by association with or reference to one of the 'great' players on his instrument ('he plays like...' is enough to establish all that needs to be known about a new musician.) In fact it is common in jazz to find exact, identical in every detail, replicas of well-known stylists. Nobody is fooled, of course, by these imitations except, possibly, the mimic[1] but it is a situation which is generally accepted and considered as normal: a huge proportion of the music played is almost totally derivative.

This situation, which can be one of the main drawbacks in any improvised music, stems, of course, from practices which are an intrinsic part of it. Firstly, the learning method in any idiomatic improvisation does have obvious dangers. It is clear that the three stages – choosing a master, absorbing his skills through practical imitation, developing an individual style and attitude from that foundation – have a tendency, very often, to be reduced to two stages with the hardest step, the last one, omitted. Imitating the style and instrumental habits of a famous player who is in all probability a virtuoso is not necessarily an easy matter and, successfully achieved, is an accomplishment which can supply a musician with considerable satisfactions; not the least of which is the admiration of those musicians less successfully attempting the same thing. In jazz, to say that someone 'sounds just like' a well-known somebody is usually meant as a compliment. So the pressure to conform, to be no more than a very good imitator is considerable. The second danger is in the search for authenticity.

For a performer, a concern for authenticity most easily avoids deteriorating into formalism when its expression is unselfconscious, but the main corrective is provided by the naturally innovative or developmental side of improvisation. When the balance between these two forces – a regard for the authenticity of the music and the intrinsically explorative nature of improvisation – is disturbed, the effect is to drag the music one way or the other, to take it in purely innovative directions or to lead it into unconscious self-parody.

Something undeniably went wrong with the balance in jazz. Increasingly, development became the preserve of a minute body of 'innovators.' For the rest the only game was follow the leader.

---

1 There is an unlikely-sounding but probably true story about Lester Young. One of his admirers, a tenor player whose style of playing was based exclusively on Lester's, made the pilgrimage to listen to his idol. Young, a musician of beautiful unpredictability, very rare in jazz, produced a quite uncharacteristic performance. The disciple, enraged, shouted at him 'You ain't you, I'm you'.

JAZZ

(2)

The American soprano saxophonist Steve Lacy, like many jazzmen in recent years, has chosen Europe as the base for his activities, first living in Italy and subsequently Paris. During the 1950s and early '60s he lived in New York and at that time took part in many of the developments and changes then taking place – events which led to what was later called 'free jazz'.

I suggested to Steve Lacy that the extreme changes that came about in the late '50s and early '60s were possibly due to an increase in self-consciousness on the part of jazz musicians, an increase in artistic self-awareness.

Of course, the thing comes more to the surface. The longer you do something the more aware you become of it. That's inevitable, and you lose your innocence, collectively and individually. And you lose your youth and the music loses its youth.

We discussed how jazz in earlier times didn't seem too concerned with its past – its 'roots'. It seemed more of a totally contemporary activity.

For me that's where the music always has to be – on the edge – in between the known and the unknown and you have to keep pushing it towards the unknown otherwise it and you die. The changes which began in the late '50s and were probably completed by the middle '60s came about because in the '50s jazz was no longer on the edge. When you reach what was called 'hard bop' there was no mystery any more. It was like – mechanical – some kind of gymnastics. The patterns are well-known and everybody is playing them. When I was coming up in New York in the '50s I was always into the radical players but at the same time I was contemporary with some of the younger accepted players. And sometimes I would go up and play with them. People like Donald Byrd and Herbie Hancock. They were the newer accepted people. I was also working with Cecil Taylor, Mal Waldron and other people who were the radicals. I was really mainly concerned to work with the radical people but at the same time I couldn't ignore the non-radical elements. But for me playing with the accepted people never worked out. Simply because they knew all the patterns and I didn't. And I knew what it took to learn them but I just didn't have the stomach for it. I didn't have the appetite. Why should I want to learn all those trite patterns? You know, when Bud Powell made them, fifteen years earlier, they weren't patterns. But when somebody analysed them and put them into a system it became a school and many players joined it. But by the time I came to it, I saw through it – the thrill was gone. Jazz got so that it wasn't improvised any more. A lot of the music that was going on was really not improvised. It got so that everybody knew what was going to happen and, sure enough, that's what happened. Maybe the order of the phrases and tunes would be a little different every night, but for me that wasn't enough. It reached a point where I, and many other people, got sick and tired of the 'beat' and the '4 bars' – everybody got tired of the systematic playing, and we just said 'Fuck it'.

But I think the question of appetite is very important. Some people are of a progressive bent and some are not. And you can't ask either of them to change. Some people are interested in carrying on an old tradition and they can find their kicks in shifting round patterns and they are not in any rush to find new stuff. They can rummage around the old stuff all their lives. People become obsessed with not just maintaining a tradition but with perfecting it. Some people search for the perfect arrangement of the old patterns and that is progress for them. Other people want to beat down the walls and find some new territory.

What Cecil Taylor was doing started in the early '50s. And the results were as free as anything you could hear. But it was not done in a free way. It was built up very, very systematically but with a new ear and new values. But there was complete opposition to what he was doing in the '50s. To me in New York he was the most important figure in the earlier '50s. Then when Ornette hit town, that was the blow. On the one hand there were all the academic players, the hard-boppers, the 'Blue-Note' people, the 'Prestige' people, and they were doing stuff which had slight progressive tendencies in it. But when Ornette hit the scene, that was the end of the theories. He destroyed the theories. I remember at that time he said, very carefully, 'Well, you just have a certain amount of space and you put what you want in it'. And that was a revelation. And we used to listen to him and Don Cherry every night and that really spread a thirst for more freedom.

But I think the key figure just then was Don Cherry. Cherry was freer, in a way. He didn't worry about all the stuff that Ornette was worrying about and his playing was really free. He used to come over to my house in '59 and '60, around that time, and he used to tell me, 'Well, let's play'. So I said 'OK. What shall we play'. And there it was. The dilemma. The problem. It was a terrible moment. I didn't know what to do. And it took me about five years to work myself out of that. To break through that wall. It took a few years to get to the point where I could just play.

It was a process that was partly playing tunes and playing tunes and finally getting to the point where it didn't seem to be important and it didn't do

55

anything for you, to play the tunes. So you just drop the tunes. And you just played. It happened in gradual stages. There would be a moment here, a fifteen minutes there, a half hour there, an afternoon, an evening, and then all the time. And then it stayed that way for a couple of years. No tunes, nothing. Just get up and play. But it all had a lot to do with the musical environment. You have to get some kindred spirits. And at the time that was in the air. It was happening everywhere. But I think that jazz, from the time it first began, was always concerned with degrees of freedom. The way Louis Armstrong played was 'more free' than earlier players. Roy Eldridge was 'more free' than his predecessors, Dizzy Gillespie was another stage and Cherry was another. And you have to keep it going otherwise you lose that freedom. And then the music is finished. It's a matter of life and death. The only criterion is: 'Is this stuff alive or is it dead?'

The revolution that was free jazz is long over and a process variously described as maturing, re-trenchment, rationalisation, consolidation – all the usual euphemisms for a period of stagnation and reaction – has turned much of free jazz into a music as formal, as ritualised and as un-free, as any of the music against which it rebelled. Like the rest of jazz it now seems to have very little existence outside the perennial festivals at which it presents its stars demonstrating whatever it was that made them stars. But in these situations free jazz seems to fulfil a somewhat peripheral role and has never managed to integrate in any way with the main body of jazz which, after first greeting the free development with scorn and vituperation, has ever since contrived to ignore it.

In recent years there has been a movement towards a new conception of jazz as 'black classical music'. Stemming from attitudes held in free jazz the intention is, I think, to cover the whole of jazz with this label. In many respects it seems an appropriate move as increasingly jazz assumes the postures and attitudes of white classical music, more and more it becomes a clearly defined rigid music, self-consciously insisting on a set of values and judgements by which it can assess not only itself but everything around it. Increasingly it displays an obsession with its own antecedents and a concern that its practice and its past should be institutionalised in conservatory and museum. There's a desire to present to the world a respectable 'official' face authenticated by a phalanx of academics and propagandists, an authority to counter-balance the institutional and academic authority of white classical music. These are strange ambitions in a music which once so clearly demonstrated the empty fatuity of all these things.

A couple of by-products of jazz's retreat into academicism are an increase in the sort of critical rhetoric which, to quote Duke Ellington, 'stinks the place up', and a greater divisiveness in a music already prone to factionalism.

Anthony Braxton, who works, as did many of his great predecessors, to extend his tradition and not merely to celebrate it, has been at various times a favourite target of the propagandists, attacking him for: betraying his race (as was Louis Armstrong); being an intellectual (as was Charlie Parker); and diluting the musical purity of his tradition (as was John Coltrane). In short, he stands accused of just about all those things which have previously served to enrich and strengthen jazz. Braxton, recognised by the musicians who work with him as an outstanding musical figure, is unlikely to be deflected by this sort of stuff but if jazz no longer values the sort of qualities he represents then it has a pretty arid future.

Fortunately, jazz has always had its share of unruly spirits, players unconstrained by either prevailing fashion or any single imposed aesthetic. Cecil Taylor, almost forty years after his first explorations and discoveries, still looks to expand his playing horizons and, showing the courage which has been evident throughout his career, continues to seek out new situations and musical challenges. But of young players seeking adventure, there's little sign.

* * *

In 1990, I had an opportunity talk with Max Roach about some of these things. As one of the founding fathers of modern jazz drumming and no stranger to any of the succeeding frontiers of jazz development, he very much represents one of the older jazz traditions, that of innovation. I put it to him that the apparently inexhaustible succession of innovators which characterised jazz in its earlier days appears to have dried up. He responded in a way which, I think, typifies the present attitude in jazz to such a question. He ignored it, pointing instead to the perceived advantages in the present situation, the wealth of the legacy which is now available to jazz musicians.

This music, which has been developing throughout the twentieth century, really excites me. Especially when I know that I can go all the way back with, say, New Orleans music and on up to Cecil Taylor and enjoy it all and get so much out of it. And it all stems from improvisation.

And for Steve Lacy, a musician who has always valued independence and freedom, the commitment to jazz through improvisation remains unchanged.

I'm attracted to improvisation because of something I value. That is a freshness, a certain quality, which can only be obtained by improvisation, something you cannot possibly get from writing. It is something to do with the 'edge'. Always being on the brink of the unknown and being prepared for the leap. And when you go on out there you have all your years of preparation and all your sensibilities and your prepared means but it is a leap into the unknown. If through that leap you find something then it has a value which I don't think can be found in any other way. I place a higher value on that than on what you can prepare. But I am also hooked into what you can prepare, especially in the way that it can take you to the edge. What I write is to take you to the edge safely so that you can go on out there and find this other stuff. But really it is this other stuff that interests me and I think it forms the basic stuff of jazz.

Sonny Rollins (Caroline Forbes)

Ronnie Scott (Val Wilmer)

Steve Lacy and Evan Parker (Caroline Forbes)

Louis Armstrong (Val Wilmer)

Max Roach (Val Wilmer)

Anthony Pay (Caroline Forbes)

John Zorn (Caroline Forbes)

Tony Oxley, Hugh Metcalf, Phil Wachsmann, and Wolfgang Fuchs
(Caroline Forbes)

Derek Bailey (Courtesy The British Library)

Gavin Bryars (Caroline Forbes)

John Stevens (Caroline Forbes)

Han Bennink (Caroline Forbes)

PART FOUR

The Composer

'...the subject of Sir Gawain and The Green Knight was chosen because, after thinking about it for thirty years or so, he now felt ready to deal musically with Gawain's confrontation with his real self.'

The larger part of classical composition is closed to improvisation and, as its antithesis, it is likely that it will always remain closed. But, starting in the early 1950s, there have been continuing attempts to re-integrate improvisation and composition. Mainly this has been through a broadening of the concept and role of notation. In the past, the main means by which improvisation was restricted and removed was through the development of notation, a process here described by Jacques Charpentier: 'When, at the end of the Middle Ages, the Occident attempted to notate musical discourse, it was actually only a sort of shorthand to guide an accomplished performer, who was otherwise a musician of oral and traditional training. These graphic signs were sufficiently imprecise to be read only by an expert performer and sufficiently precise to help him find his place if, by mishap, he had a slip of memory. Consequently, as we see, it was not a question of precise notation but rather a mnemonic device in written symbols. Later on, the appearance of the musical staff on the one hand, and symbols of time duration on the other, made it possible to move on to real notation which reflects with exactitude the whole of the musical material presented in this manner. At this point in history it does not seem as if the contemporaries of that time fully realised the consequences of their discovery. For in actual fact, from that moment on, a musical work was no longer strictly musical; it existed outside itself, so to speak, in the form of an object to which a name was given: the score. The score very soon ceased to be the mere perpetuator of a tradition, to become the instrument of elaboration of the musical work itself. Consequently the analytical qualities of musical discourse took precedence in the course of centuries over its qualities of synthesis and the musical work ceased to be, little by little, the expression of an experienced psycho-physiological continuum – on the spot and at the moment it is experienced; and instead became what is more and more prevalent today in the Occident – that is a wilful, formal and explicative construction which finds in itself alone its substance and its justification.'

The efforts in recent times to loosen the stranglehold that notation came to have on the music came partly through a re-introduction of a certain amount of flexibility in the role of the performer, providing him with the possibility of affecting the creation of the music during its performance. Some of these developments, while removing some degree of control from the composer, have not necessarily introduced the possibility of improvisation. But there are composers who have deliberately turned towards improvisation. Earle Brown, the American composer, was possibly the first to move in this direction. His notation is here described by Morton Feldman: 'The sound is placed in its approximate visual relationship to that which surrounds it. Time is not indicated mechanistically, as with rhythm. It is articulated for the performer but not interpreted. The effect is twofold.

'When the performer is made more intensely aware of time, he also becomes more intensely aware of the action or sound he is about to play. The result is a heightened spontaneity which only performance itself can convey. Brown's notation, in fact, is geared to counteract just this discrepancy between the written page and the realities of performance.'

His 'time notation', however, was only one reflection of Earle Brown's interest in improvisation. He described to me how

...in 1952 when I was experimenting with open form and aspects of improvisation, my influences to do that were primarily from the American sculptor Alexander Calder and the mobiles, which are transforming works of art, I mean they have indigenous transformational factors in their construction, and this seemed to me to be just beautiful. As you walk into a museum and you look at a mobile you see a configuration that's moving very subtly. You walk in the same building the next day and its a different configuration, yet it's the same piece, the same work by Calder. It took me a couple of years to figure out how to go about it musically. I thought that it would be fantastic to have a piece of music which would have a basic character always, but by virtue of aspects of improvisation or notational flexibility, the piece could take on subtly different kinds of character.

Indeterminate composition, which might be described as any kind of composition in which the composer deliberately relinquishes control of any element of the composition, seems to be concerned with utilising two quite different concepts; aleatoric and improvisation. I asked Earle Brown what, for him, was the difference between them.

Well, aleatory is a word that Boulez used in an article a long time ago which means throwing of dice and so forth. It's really chance, and I am vehemently against considering improvisation as chance music... Cage was literally flipping coins to decide which sound event was to follow which sound

event and that was to remove his choice, his sense of choice, and it was also not to allow the musician to have any choice either, and I was not interested in that at all. At the same time that he was organising strictly and fixedly by chance process, I was working with improvisational forms.

In the Universal Edition score (no.15306) of his String Quartet (1965), Earle Brown writes:

I have fixed the overall form but have left areas of flexibility within the inner structures.

And among the directions for performance is:

The relative pitch duration and rhythm are indicated by the graphics, and the instrumental techniques are given – only the precise 'pitches' are left to the discretion of the performers. (This has been aptly described as an 'action notation'; the actual pitches sounded are a function of accurately performing what has been given.) All four parts are included in each part so that an eye-ear ensemble is possible.

More radically his instructions for the last, the 'open form', section of the work are:

There are 8 or 10 events for each musician, separated from one another by vertical dotted lines. Each musician may play any of his events at any time, in any order and at any speed. In some cases the technique, the loudness and/or the rhythm may be 'free' for the individual musician to determine; where these elements are given they must be observed. All of the materials in these events have appeared previously in the work, but not necessarily in the part in which they appear in this section. This section is, in effect, a free coda, to be assembled spontaneously by the quartet. The section includes very articulate materials, 'below-bridge' sounds, and sustained sounds. These can be spontaneously assembled in any sequence and position; but through sensitive ensemble listening I believe that spontaneous 'rational' continuities of techniques will arise. So that, for instance, a statistical area of inarticulate sounds moving into a 'below-bridge' area, into an area of primarily articulate material...or any other sequence of statistical similarities of texture and style is created. I prefer that such 'ordering' should come about in this intuitive-conscious manner spontaneously during each performance. A complete pre-performance ordering of these materials – which I could very well arrange myself – would eliminate the possibility of the intense, immediate communication of ensemble collaboration which is an extremely important aspect of 'music-making' as I see it.

Having passed over some control to the musicians, how much did Earle Brown want to retain? I quoted an instruction from the score of the Quartet, 'Play events between dotted lines in any order independently, conscious of ensemble'. There are a number of possible interpretations of 'conscious of ensemble', aren't there? I can think of musicians who are only happy in an ensemble they dominate.

I know. That's one of the ego problems that you are confronted with in some situations, but basically, you know, it's always a collaborative thing of give and take, and what I expect is goodwill. I got to doing that quartet thing after a great deal of experience. In 1952 I went to the extreme of very, very tenuous vague suggestions of actions – the next stop beyond that would have been a blank page, but we all have blank pages anyway, and I don't need to give anybody a blank page. On the other hand, within the same year, 1952, I'd done absolutely strict, totally organised, serial music. And so I was seeing from both directions, from the extremes, the degrees of flexibility that I could dictate through notation, and the degrees of control I could imply through very vague indications. And I also had come up as a jazz musician – and also the influence of Alexander Calder and Jackson Pollock's paintings... Jackson was sort of a wild guy and he was a very brilliant man and felt this kind of intensity in his own spontaneity and it occurred to me that Jackson was almost performing his paintings – and so all of these things came together in 1951 and '52 for me and I produced this thing which I called Experiments in Notation, Performance Process – what the human mind does when it is confronted with graphic stimuli or literal notation. These qualities of control interested me.

The main difference that occurs to me between your methods and Jackson Pollock's is that you are using other people's sensibilities, other people's spontaneity, and with Jackson Pollock, of course, his involvement was direct. You are accepting the effect of the situation on other people's sensibilities.

Yes, but you see it's my responsibility to try and condition their sensibility involvement. I used to envy painters very much because they had their work in their hands, so to speak. They could see it. When you've done it, it's in its real form. Writing music you don't have the real thing. All you have are symbols. So, in any case, the writing of music involves an aspect of projection, I would say, projecting your imagination into a situation you are not going to be present in, and in that sense it's not so strange for me to try to project one stage further, which is to project the conditions that I hope, with good will, the musicians will enter into.

So the responsibility of the performers is still entirely to the composer – just as if they were going to play a fully notated piece?

I think so...but what I say is that I am extending an invitation to the musicians to take part with me.

Do you have difficulties with improvisors who have developed their playing within one particular style? I mean if you gave a piece of graphic notation to one clarinet player it might come out sounding like New Orleans jazz and the same part played by another clarinet player might sound like Mozart.

Yes, I'm not really sure I'm wanting to produce stylistic collisions... You see, it is somewhat my responsibility to create conditions which, in a certain sense, won't be violated stylistically. For instance, if there's somebody who is very good at improvising in the style of Bach, or in the baroque period, very often I suggest something verbally. Like, I ask for erratic, jagged rhythms, so that he would not make sequences of 8th notes.

Well possibly there's some advantage then in having a musician who doesn't have a stylistic commitment? Who possibly doesn't improvise?

Improvising takes a certain degree of self-confidence and a lot of classical musicians don't have that self-confidence. But the people for whom I write, leading groups who are interested in avant garde music, already have approached that, they've experienced it, they've heard other people do it and they are aware of those problems. In 1952 I was convinced that music, our music, was going to move in a certain way which would be more inclusive of flexibility, let us say, and it has moved in that direction. In the string quartet there is an improvised ending but they have certain controls in there, they are given a repertoire of material. If the Budapest String Quartet, say, were to play the end of my quartet with those materials already mentioned I think that they would do it very well, if it interested them, but, if I had not written those materials, I would probably be dissatisfied with the results. They would start quoting the repertoire they know best and I've always tried to provoke the musician to go beyond his habits.

I suppose all composition in the past has produced the performer it needs and I suppose there are now more musicians who give you the type of interpretation you want?

Oh yes, it's progressively easier and easier for me to get good performances.

* * *

One of the things that has come up repeatedly with people who have spoken about their improvisation is the term *duende*. Paco Peña, the flamenco guitar player, described how there are times when the singer and the dancer and the guitarist combine to achieve a new level of performance and they call that duende. I wondered if you were interested, in your composition, in increasing the possibility of duende?

Yes, absolutely. Sometimes I conduct these improvisational works, and in a sense, I am conducting spontaneously – selecting timbres from the group, you know? ... It's one of the reasons I started using graphic notations and some degree of improvisation. I remember John Cage when he was doing his – I mean he's still doing it – chance music where he flipped coins and got sequences of things and then they were performed by a stopwatch...after chance had made the arrangement, the way of performing it was with a stopwatch. One minute, thirty-three seconds somebody goes 'chic-boom', forty-four seconds later an instrument goes 'blup'. I sat through a lot of concerts of chance music, my own and other people's, and I really felt that was a very cold thing, you know?

Very anti-duende, I should think.

And because they were organised by chance the continuity was very strange so they were in one sense very good. But they were the antithesis of what I was interested in, which is performer intensity; the relationship of one person to another... I wanted to give the musician a little breathing space. I guess I like that feeling of space, flexing, breathing, you know?

I would have thought that to give the performer more space and flexibility was a particularly apt thing to do since the introduction of electronic music, which actually does give a composer the chance to realise his compositions absolutely accurately. The availability of that technology seems to set the performer apart in a way – release him. If you want complete discipline – absolute accuracy – your best field would be electronics, perhaps.

But you see, most every composer who was into electronic music early – the others would have to tell you what they think – but for me I believe that we all felt the kind of coldness in this thing. And for my part I found it very boring just to sit down in the studio and cut and splice tape and combine these things. I mean I really like the society of making music with people, you know? And that's what I try and create in my scoring.

Before the end of our conversation I asked Earle Brown about a forthcoming concert of his music to be performed in Rotterdam, in which fully notated pieces and *December '52*, an almost totally improvised piece, were to be performed by the same musicians. What sort of problems did he expect?

Well, in a certain sense, I have to teach improvisation every time I do that piece with different people... I must teach the nature of the piece and create a mental and sonic condition for the piece.

Nevertheless, I believe affirmatively that improvisation is a musical art which passed out of Western usage for a time but is certainly back now. And I felt that it would come back which is why I based a lot of my work on certain aspects of it. It's here and I think it's going to stay. And it's not going to do away with the writing of music but it's going to bring an added dimension – of aliveness – to a composition and bring the musician into a greater intensity of working on that piece.

THE COMPOSER AND THE NON-IMPROVISOR

As improvisation is present to some degree in almost all musical activities it would seem that the ability to improvise might be a basic part of every player's musicianship. There are, however, musicians who not only cannot improvise but to whom the whole activity is incomprehensible. As might be expected, the non-improvisor is usually to be found in classical music, but he can even be found in areas of music where improvisation plays an integral part. A high measure of skill in other aspects of instrumental playing is no guarantee of the ability to improvise. Earle Brown: 'As a matter of fact, some of the most brilliant performers on instruments go completely dead if you ask them to imagine something.'

The *Grove Dictionary of Music and Musicians* (1954), which defines improvisation as 'The art of thinking and performing music simultaneously', seems by implication rather unkind to the non-improvisor. Stephen Hicks, the organist, didn't believe in him. 'If they have absolute control and a real knowledge of harmony then, with practice, anyone can improvise.' Steve Howe pointed to a disadvantage shared by most non-improvisors: 'If they've had classical training they usually can't improvise...because they can't see into it, you know, how simple it really is.'

Any sort of strict classical training does seem to be the biggest single handicap to improvising. The standard instrumental technique itself probably contains certain disadvantages but the main block is the instilled attitude towards music-making which seems to automatically accompany this type of education. An attitude which could not appreciate something like: 'You hear people trying out things, they make a mistake and they perhaps even develop that mistake and work out something nice from that which happened without them meaning it to.' Paco Peña here does not indicate any lack of responsibility towards the music he plays or any reduced concern for the quality of the performance. He is expressing a recognition that music is, of its nature, not fixed and is always malleable, changeable. Performance in classical music seems designed to disprove that idea. In the straight world the performer approaches music on tiptoe. Music is precious and performance constitutes a threat to its existence. So, of course, he has to be careful. Also, the music doesn't belong to him. He's allowed to handle it but then only under the strictest supervision. Somebody, somewhere, has gone through a lot of trouble to create this thing, this composition, and the performer's primary responsibility is to preserve it from damage. At its highest, music is a divine ideal conceived by a super-mortal. In which case performance becomes a form of genuflection.

It is undeniable that for many musicians, performing music is a matter of being a highly skilled executant in a well-rehearsed ensemble, and it is also true that this role has its satisfactions. But it does seem that to be trained solely for that role is probably the worst possible preparation for improvisation. And the biggest handicap inflicted by that training is the instilling of a deeply reverential attitude towards the creation of music, an attitude which unquestioningly accepts the physical and hierarchical separation of playing and creating. From this stems the view of improvisation as a frivolous or even a sacrilegious activity.

Perhaps none of this would matter if it were not that musicians with this sort of background are sometimes asked to improvise. Fortunately, there are very few composers naïve enough to instruct the normal symphony orchestra to improvise – certainly I don't think any of them ever try it twice. But even members of specialist new music ensembles very often bring to improvising no preparation or training other than what they have received for orchestral playing – an utterly alien activity. These specialist ensembles, mentioned earlier by Earle Brown, are usually made up of musicians with a conventional orchestral background and training but who have a particular interest in new music and the instrumental techniques and developments associated with it. They do not necessarily have any knowledge of, or even interest in, improvisation.

Anthony Pay, the distinguished clarinettist, who at the time of our conversation was with the London Sinfonietta, had never improvised and probably never considered improvising until confronted with the necessity to do so in his work with the Sinfonietta. He described for me some of the problems he had experienced in this situation.

You see, when you play modern music you often come upon very difficult technical situations. You might be asked to play complicated rhythms. You might be asked to play things the execution of which demands complete concentration, and I am the sort of player who is more disposed to start off from the accuracy point of view rather than starting off from the musical point of view. You can, with some modern music, start off and say: 'I'm not going to pay a tremendous amount of attention to the notational aspects of it, but initially I'm going to decide what the music is about, the gestures – and language – the sort of thing that, if you are improvising, you have to deal with.' Now, I tend, when I'm approaching a modern score, to start off by trying to get, as accurately as I can, what he's actually put down on paper. And that can be, as I say, very constricting. If you are trying to play seven against nine or something like that then you can be involved in thoughts which aren't specially musical ones. I don't think I'd ever appreciated the sort of thing that could come out of improvisation before I was involved with Stockhausen. I don't think that there are many contemporary scores which require total improvisation. People who do improvisation are generally outstanding performers who are interested in improvisation and who do it in an exclusive sort of way. And it is true that people who are good at improvisation need not necessarily be very good at realising what a composer actually intends in a precisely notated work, and the difficulty comes when you have to mix these two things.

As you have no improvising background, where, in the absence of specific instructions from the composer, does your material come from? The jazz musician, say, in your position might draw on his usual improvising vocabulary (which might or might not suit the composer). Where would you look for your material?

Well it's not precisely clear where I do look for it. Perhaps I just let it happen. Perhaps you just wait and you listen as closely as possible to whatever is going on and you just react. Of course, that is why group improvisation is much easier to do. Because then you can listen to what happens and you can try and contribute to what is going on, or you can try to destroy what's going on. Those are two goals that you can consider.

It might be thought that in interpretation the non-improvisor might be dealing with musical matters close to the heart of improvisation. But one of the main differences between interpretation and improvisation was pointed out by Anthony Pay.

There is a crucial difference in terms of the way in which performers approach music. If you are playing in a symphony orchestra or if you are playing a piece of chamber music, you are trying, often against fairly heavy odds, to find out what somebody has meant when they said something. And I think that a jazz player, for example, is saying what is in him. He puts very much more of his total personality into what he does. I think he's a much happier individual in many ways.

What is the main difference that you find between playing strictly notated music and improvising? Do you deliberately loosen certain standards of accuracy, or something like that, when you turn to improvisation?

Technically there are a tremendous number of things from which you are immediately liberated. For example, precise pitch; you can bend notes around all over the place, you can get microtonal effects. You can play practically inaudibly and you don't feel that you are doing a disservice to something. But I think for me truly to assess what improvisation will be for me I would have to spend quite a long time doing it with a few people who I felt had the same sort of ideas and did the same sort of things. It's always noticeable that there is someone who doesn't quite do the sort of things that you want him to do — whether it's playing Mozart or Brahms or whatever — and I just think that that is also true of improvisation. You can't just throw a group of people together and get it right. And I think that is something I ought to concentrate on for my own development as a musician. The difference is, as far as I am concerned, that one is unknown poetry in which I can progress. In playing written, precisely notated music I'm not actually progressing. I'm just learning to do better what I already do.

THE COMPOSER – IN PRACTICE

(1)

The unique experience for a composer in the use of improvisation must be the relinquishing of control over at least some of the music and, even more critically for the composer, passing over that control not to 'chance' but to other musicians. Earle Brown in *1952* gave, as he says, 'almost a blank page to the musicians', and his object in doing that was to investigate performance procedures. In that particular case presumably whatever the musicians played would be acceptable as data for those investigations. However, in most of its uses by composers improvisation is employed for more precise compositional aims. In other words, what the improvisors play is of great importance indeed to the composer. Usually, he has specific musical expectations of the improvisors, and their inventions are required to serve his predetermined ends. Anthony Pay:

One sort of improvisation that we can be called upon to do is when composers want a certain sort of texture at some point and then they will give you a thing called the box technique, and composers have used this quite frequently. What happens is that you're given a box in which there are a number of notes, and you're asked to improvise upon those particular notes. The unfortunate thing about that is that it does tend to always sound pretty much the same. People have developed a kind of technique for dealing with that sort of thing, and it very rarely has a very clear relationship to the idiom of the work involved. It's a useful technique to provide a sort of sound ambience – I think its a device which composers have used to try and get away from the complications which arise when you try to notate things which don't actually coincide. If you start writing fives and sevens and nines so that people don't play things together then it creates complications.

One of the most active composers in this area during the 1960s and '70s was Karlheinz Stockhausen. Anthony Pay, as a member of the London Sinfonietta, worked with Stockhausen on a number of his pieces. Here he describes rehearsing Stockhausen's *Ylem* with the composer.

This piece had a clearly defined structure – it was concerned with mirroring the contraction and the expansion of the universe – which meant that the durations of the improvisations and so on were precisely controlled. It started off with very, very fast repeated notes, all of which got slower and slower and the ranges within which these notes were confined go wider and wider so that you found yourself not only playing notes which were central in the range of your instrument but which become higher and lower. And as the range got wider the time between each attack of these notes got longer and longer and, in fact, at the centre point of the piece the time between each attack was a minute and a half. Stockhausen said, you must only play for a fifth of the interval of attack (approximately 18 seconds) so that there is more silence than playing. By that time, of course, you couldn't be just playing a single note. You had to be playing something which was centred on a single pitch so that your improvisation had – not a tonal centre – a sort of note centre. When we did rehearsals of this particular piece Stockhausen had a number of us play a section of the piece and then we each, individually, criticised each other's interpretation of the instructions. Somebody would say – 'You played for too long' – or – 'You always play phrases that go 'ba-bum' – and so on.

I asked if there was any attempt to get an idiomatic consistency, to confine the music to a particular style.

Stockhausen always tried to mix free pieces with composed pieces in a concert. And that, of course, makes for a relationship between the idiom of the extemporisation and the idiom of his pieces as they are when they are precisely notated. But, in this particular piece he was after variety, you see. If it's supposed to be representative of the universe then anything goes, as it were.

So Stockhausen wouldn't have found, say, a quotation from Puccini inadmissible?

Well, yes, he did mind that sort of thing. As a matter of fact he objected to something of that sort which was played.

Would the composer's likes and dislikes be important to you in your improvisations? Although not specifically indicated in the score, would your awareness of the composer's preferences influence your choice of what to play? For instance if, for reasons which arose in the playing situation at the time, you thought it would be singularly appropriate to play something tonal would the fact that Stockhausen might not like that inhibit you?

I don't think it would inhibit me. My experiences with Stockhausen lead me to suppose that quite often he can be impressed by something that people do which is contrary to what he has suggested. There was a striking example of this in the piece Ylem *which we have been discussing. We played it, I think, seven or eight times and then we recorded it. It was late at night in an Abbey Road studio and the version we recorded lasted 22 minutes. And then we listened to it. And then we recorded another version and listened to that. Then we recorded a third version and listened to that. And then we all voted as to which version we thought was the best representation of this particular piece. Now in the middle of the second performance the trumpet player seemed to have a brainstorm. Although according to Stockhausen's instructions he was only allowed to play, in the middle of the piece, for at the most eighteen seconds out of each minute and a half, he played for thirty to thirty-five seconds then after a short pause went off again. And, although it was very inspired in many ways it was completely outside the bounds of that particular piece, and we were all flabbergasted. Well, when it came to the vote we all agreed that the third performance was the best. It was the most controlled, it had the right amount of individuality and the right amount of group spirit and everything else. But Stockhausen, after first agreeing with us, then changed his mind and said he now preferred the second version, the one in which the trumpet player had taken off. So I said, 'But that's ridiculous, we've all been rehearsing it the way you say it ought to be done, with this controlled pattern you asked for, and you pick the second version which you must agree doesn't fit into that pattern at all.' And Stockhausen said 'Yes, oh yes, but it was very interesting.' And so after writing this piece and rehearsing it for a long time to get the pattern as he wanted it, he was, nevertheless, prepared to accept the, well, the individual thing that was brought about by this trumpet player.[1]*

Would it be possible to indicate how the trumpet player had been so effective?

He made it sound not like a trumpet at all. It was most curious. He took some of the tubing out of the instrument, and he played on the mouthpiece only for part of the time. It was a remarkable demonstration. I was very annoyed at the time. I thought 'what on earth is he doing? He's completely ruined this'. And that was a reaction which, although appropriate to the way in which I was approaching the piece, wasn't necessarily the right reaction. It's very difficult to say. I mean how much are you entitled to be free with music?

Why do you think the trumpet player did that? Did he offer an explanation?

Oh, I just think he was off in his own world. Perhaps Stockhausen would say that he was in communion with the universe. Stockhausen's actual way of dealing with people can, on occasions, be very mystical. He invites you, for example, to play in the rhythm of the molecules which constitute your body. Or in the rhythm of the universe. There's a story of a second violin player who said, 'Herr Stockhausen, how will I know when I am playing in the rhythm of the universe?' Stockhausen said, with a smile, 'I will tell you'.

It might be worth noting that an Indian musician asked to play in the rhythm of the universe would immediately know what to do. The origin of the word laya – the right feel or pulse for a performance (discussed on page 4) – is

---

1 The recording discussed is on Deutsche-Grammophon 2530442.

connected with the Hindu belief in the all-embracing, comprehensive rhythm of the universe as personified in Shiva. So the Indian musician could have complied exactly with Stockhausen's instructions. That doesn't mean, of course, that what he played would have been acceptable to Stockhausen.

One of the things which quickly becomes apparent in any improvising is that one spends very little time looking for 'new' things to play. The instinctive choice as well as the calculated choice is usually for tried material. Improvisation is hardly ever deliberately experimental. When the 'new' arrives, if it arrives, it appears to come of its own accord. I asked Anthony Pay if the composer, during the seven or eight performances of *Ylem*, encouraged the players to aim for deliberately different versions?

He said to us that perhaps we should try and prepare ourselves for each performance by thinking of something that we hadn't ever done before. That after each performance we could prepare ourselves in a mental way for the next performance by thinking of something new and, perhaps, that would find its way into the context of what everyone else was doing and contribute to the piece. There are certain simple things that you can do which are always effective. You can, for instance, play a very loud, very high note at an appropriate point – that could be extremely effective. It's not precisely what you did, it was also when you did it that made it terribly appropriate. I remember in one of the recordings something amazing happened. We were playing long notes and all the wind players happened to start at one particular time and drift into a common chord and then out again. And when we listened to the playback it was a moment which was, for us, tremendously meaningful. Partly, I suppose, because it was a total accident. But I think improvising styles change very slowly in those people who have a very developed improvising style. Sometimes the strength of the way in which a player plays something lies in his depth of approach in one particular area. I think that to say that so and so always improvises in the same sort of way is not necessarily a criticism. It's often a very great strength and people can explore in depth one particular way of going about improvisation.

Anthony Pay also talked about some of the more general aspects of playing modern music.

When you are playing a lot of modern music perhaps your capacity for invention becomes stultified because, to some extent, you are reduced to being a machine in a certain sort of style. Things have become so complicated that it's difficult to get outside of the actual complications that you are trying to represent. I think it's a great advantage if we can. I mean, what makes people who can play modern music is not people who have the capacity necessarily to do the complicated things that are required of the performer but people who have a feeling for what modern music is trying to convey. There are people who seem inherently incapable of understanding what it means to play modern music. They think it's terrible, they think it has nothing to do with music, that it's unmusical, that you can't be a good musician and want to make the sort of sounds that modern music can be involved with.

I suggested that this rejection of modern music often accompanied, and was possibly caused by, an almost religious allegiance to tonality. He thought that to some extent this might be so, and continued:

I think there is a great split between musicians nowadays; between those who regard contemporary music as being largely arbitrary and basically unmusical, and those who are excited by what is actually going on. But it seems to me that musicians obviously have to be interested in what's going on. What reason has one for existing other than to be involved with what is actually being created in your particular time?

Anthony Pay summed up his attitude to the improvisor/non-improvisor question by saying:

If you can understand what it means to be disciplined and to be accurate, committed and involved with something which is purely notated, and also be capable of being free, of being able to step outside the inhibition that notation produces, and do something which is your own and relevant, then I still think that combination is probably the highest form of instrumental talent that there is. And it is only the really great instrumentalists who can do that, who are free of their instrument to that extent.

THE COMPOSER – IN PRACTICE

(2)

Since the foregoing discussions, carried out in the early 1970s, the situation in contemporary composition, as in everything else, has changed radically. 'New Music', flinching from the no-nonsense philistinism which characterised the 1980s, now has quite a different look, dressed as it is in armour which it assumes to be more appropriate to the times. Key words now are retrenchment, repetition, retrospective, revival; other key words are usually preceded by 'neo' or 'post'; overriding all: accessibility.

While these developments can hardly be expected to provide much of a stimulus for improvisation, it still seems to find a way into this music. There is evidence, even, of a more sophisticated approach, a recognition that improvisation is a creative force of incalculable power, not simply a way of achieving a more or less interesting set of instrumental devices.

John Zorn composes in a variety of contexts and genres and is perhaps best known for what have been described as 'vernacular' pieces – abrupt juxtapositions of different musics, including popular styles – a kind of live *musique concrète*. He has also written, over a number of years, a series of compositions which deal with improvisation, or more accurately, improvisors. His aim is not, as is usually the case, the realisation of a pre-ordained result through improvisation, but the stimulation, or the releasing, of the network of relationships possible between a group of players.

The following is taken from a number of conversations held in 1990 and '91. As he describes, his background is largely in improvisation:

I grew up in a scene of improvisors who over the course of the years developed personal languages on our instruments. We grew through playing with each other, listening to all kinds of music and creating a personal approach towards our instrument.. What I was really fascinated with was finding a way to harness these improvisors' talents in a compositional framework without actually hindering what they did best – which is improvising. An improvisor wants to have the freedom to do anything at any time. For a composer to give an improvisor a piece of music which said, 'play these melodies – then improvise – then play with this guy – then improvise – then play this figure – then improvise', to me, that was defeating the purpose of what these people had developed, which was a very particular way of relating

*to their instruments and to each other. And I was interested in those
relationships.*

*I don't talk about any sounds that anybody might make, I talk about the
improvisors themselves: 'you can play with this person if you chose to or in
alternation with that person. But what you play is totally up to you and who
you decide to play with is up to you.'*

*Traditionally, composers create an arc on a time line, a structure that
begins in one place, goes to a middle and then ends. I began composing my
game pieces by using a time line but abstracting everything away from sound
and talking about people.*

The series of compositions that Zorn has written dealing with improvisation are based on games or 'game plans'.

A piece like Archery, *which was done in '79, is a long list of a hundred and
thirty-odd combinations for a twelve-piece group. Where I really started
eliminating the time line, eliminating the idea that the composer has to create
in an arc, was in a piece like* Cobra *where the sequence of events can be
ordered at any time by anyone. There, I just created relationships, abstract
concepts that the players can order in any way they want, so that, at any
moment in the piece, if they want to do something like play solo or play duo, or
have the whole band play, they can actualise that.*

*My early game pieces were sports, like Lacrosse, Hockey, Pool, Fencing,
and I got bored with those and started using war games, kind of bookshelf
games. The rule books were intense, so thick, you know, and if you write the
rules out for the game* Cobra *they are impossible to decipher. But when
someone explains the practice of it, it's very simple. These games, like Cobra,
have a kind of oral tradition. I was very influenced by these complex war
games and I like the idea of the guerrilla systems in* Cobra. *Everything I
learned in my old pieces got incorporated in the next piece and so on.* Cobra *is
like the sum total of working with these game pieces.*

What John Zorn has to say about the incomprehensibility of the
instructions when written down was certainly borne out when I came to
transcribe his description('just briefly, without getting too specific') of just how
Cobra worked. But rehearsal, I found, is crucial for Zorn's piece and, echoing
something noted by Cornelius Cardew, rehearsal is a kind of training. There's
nothing specific, nobody is told what they should play, but there's a training in
how to incorporate the instructions into their playing and an investigation of
the possibilities opened up by them. Well, that's in practice. Here's what his
instructions look like written down:

*I've created a series of about twenty different systems. Each one cued by
the downbeat of a card. Any one of these basic systems can be called at any*

76

time by any one of the players at their whim. So what you get is a section lasting as long as the least patient person in the band who then says lets go somewhere else. Some of these cues are meant to create specific permutations of players like a duo or a trio. I mean they could be created by complete spontaneity in the sense that when the downbeat happens people who are playing can either stop or change their music or people who are not playing can decide to come in if they wish to. So with the downbeat there's gonna be a change but you have no idea who's gonna come in and who's not and you have no idea of what to expect and that could last for 5 seconds. Someone could give another downbeat, like the 'runner' downbeat, which is a very specific call: 'I want to play with this person'. I point to the people who are chosen at the downbeat and those people play. There's a substitute change, which means when the downbeat happens the people who are playing must stop and people who aren't playing may come in if they wish to. So you have a very clear idea who's not gonna play, then there are other calls that create games within the group. Duo games: when the card comes down anybody in the group can look at anybody else and do a duo with them but everybody is doing this simutaneously so it could be one duo at a time or it could be all 12 people playing 6 different duos simutaneously each ending at different times and then starting up new duos. Trading systems, where people toss ideas back and forth: I'll play and then the next person will play and then the next will play and then the next person and so on.

One card is music change. The group stays the same but the style of the music changes. It doesn't matter what they change it to, just as long as it changes. Or the opposite of that would be something you saw a bunch of times today: the group changes but the music stays the same. Say, if three people who aren't playing raise their hands and people who are playing choose them to imitate their sounds. Then at the downbeat we actualise that. Then there are memory systems – ways of when you hear something you like, it's logged into a memory and then recalled later...

It's true I pick the bands and in that sense the Ellington tradition, the selection of the people, is very important. Everybody is vital. You take one person out and the chemistry is going to be different. Its like that with choosing bands for these game pieces. You need people who are aggressive, you need people who are going to be docile, you need people with a sense of humour, you need people who are assholes, you need a wide variety to really get the piece going and picking musicians for the most part is not so much 'I need a violin and I need a cello and I need a keyboard and I need a guitar', its more the people themselves that are important.

I basically create a small society and everybody finds their own position in that society. It really becames like a psycho drama. People are given power and it's very interesting to see which people like to run away from it, who are very docile and just do what they are told, others try very hard to get more control and more power. So it's very much like the political arena in a certain kind of sense.

Some players are really kind of conceptual, thinking about structuring a piece of music, using these signals and trying to create some kind of compositional flow in their heads spontaneously. While others are, you know, creating problems. I think I am that kind of player. Bill Frisell is the kind of player who sits back and lets everybody else make decisions and just plays his butt off. Ultimately he was the one that was making the sound of the music while other people were dealing with the structure of it. Those are all valid positions to be in in the society that exists on stage when these pieces happen.

THE COMPOSER – IN QUESTION

The debate about how composition can best utilise improvisation, while of interest to the composers concerned, is of only peripheral interest, not to say irrelevant, to some players. These players consider improvisation to be an activity which has no necessary connection with composition at all. As Earle Brown says, 'we all have blank pages', and there are some of us who prefer filling our blank pages with our own signs rather than with those of other people. But we are a minority. Most improvisors do both.

Here are two different views expressed by experienced improvisors about working both under the direction of a score, and also without a score – in the free situation. Both musicians have a central interest in improvisation. The first sees advantages and validity in a collaboration between composer and improvisor and the second considers it mainly disadvantageous and limiting for the improvisor. They are both discussing working with the type of composition in which the performer is called upon to provide all aspects of the music.

Hugh Davies, improvisor, instrument-maker and composer, is discussing the performance of a piece by Stockhausen, for whom he worked for many years. It is 'Intensitat' from *Aus den Sieben Tagen* and it is a so-called text-piece. The total information available to the players is:

for ensemble
INTENSITY
play single sounds
with such dedication
until you feel the warmth
that radiates from you
play on and sustain it
as long as you can[1]

Hugh Davies: *Nothing more is given. Looking at the elements of this text that relate to musical structures and procedures, at the beginning it has 'play single sounds'. For each sound a player may choose to play a texture more complex than a single pitch, which in some cases may become almost a phrase (the same German word is deliberately translated in some texts by 'sound' and in others*

---

1 Printed by kind permission of Universal Edition.

by 'tone/note'). The continuation, 'with such dedication/until you feel the warmth/that radiates from you', implies a development of this basic element, including the probability that the performers will individually introduce new elements from time to time, but always with the tendency towards increasing the intensity of their play and their involvement in the production of each sound. Finally 'play on and sustain it/as long as you can' gives an indication of the way in which the performance ends, which is likely to be either an abrupt halt by the whole ensemble while at full strength or a fairly rapid dying away as the musicians end one after another. No direct co-ordination between the players is mentioned.

Performing such a piece, especially in an ensemble that works together regularly and specialises in such areas of music, one is very conscious of playing a definite composition, even though the nature of it is such that one need only think the text over quietly to oneself before starting to play, and then everything happens intuitively – one need not be fully conscious of what one is playing, one 'becomes the music'. In many ways this is very close to a group improvisation, with the difference that – in spite of frequent comments from various quarters about the performers and not the composers being the ones who should collect the performing right fees for such music – one remains aware of the composer influencing the performance from a distance through his score. And the structural indications in the score discussed above ensure that those elements at least will make the result completely different from a free improvisation.

* * *

Evan Parker, the saxophonist, who must be one of the most widely experienced musicians in the performing of 'composed' open form improvisation and also in 'free' open form improvisation, gave his views on this subject in an address to the Society for the Promotion of New Music. The following is an excerpt:

I am a performing musician, but I don't use scores and it's not that the score has refined itself out of existence, as Werner Goldschmidt seemed to think was the case for the New Phonic Arts Group. It has never existed for me except as something to look at and think about, to compare with others of its type. Now that I am forced to rationalise this attitude, it is along these lines: if the score represents some kind of ideal performance why does it ever have to be performed? Surely it would be better for the music-lover to read the score, alone or with others, conducted or unconducted as his preference dictates? If it is objected that this attitude is too unemotional, then I would reply that the score is itself too unemotional; and since it concerns itself with the description

80

rather than the emotions themselves it would be more appropriate to consider score-making as an esoteric branch of the literary arts with its own criteria rather than as anything to do with music. In fact I think that this possibility has already been noted and acted on by some score-makers. That symphony of Nam-June Paik's for example, where some of the durations are measured in hundreds of years. It's a very beautiful score to read... Everyone can recognise differences between the score and the performance. Things are added, altered or taken away. While this has presumably always been the case, the gap between score and performance is perhaps wider in much contemporary music than ever before. Aloys Kontarsky's comments on the contrast between the austerity of an Earle Brown score which contained only black horizontal and vertical blocks and lines and its performance in Darmstadt are very interesting: 'So the performance contained trills, glissandi, crescendi, sforzati and even all kinds of solo licks which could not have been derived with even the best of intentions from the scanty design on the page.' Leaving aside the score as the embodiment of an ideal performance, a score can also be considered a recipe for possible music-making. That's an idea I can have much more sympathy with, taking into account as it does much more than the composer and his muse. Other ingredients that a composer with this attitude might include are: performability, how much rehearsal time, which musicians will be playing the piece, where it will be played, even possibly how the audience might react. Nonetheless the most careful consideration of all the unknowns before the event cannot guarantee that the music will fit the occasion. There will still be some slack to be taken up between what the score says and what it means.

I suppose the implication in all this is obvious. I'm suggesting that if anyone in the production of a music event is dispensable, it is the score-maker, or the 'composer' as he is often called. My 'ideal music' is played by groups of musicians who choose one another's company and who improvise freely in relation to the precise emotional, acoustic, psychological and other less tangible atmospheric conditions in effect at the time the music is played.

PART FIVE

FREE

Freely improvised music, variously called 'total improvisation', 'open improvisation', 'free music', or perhaps most often simply, 'improvised music', suffers from – and enjoys – the confused identity which its resistance to labelling indicates. It is a logical situation: freely improvised music is an activity which encompasses too many different kinds of players, too many different attitudes to music, too many different concepts of what improvisation is, even, for it all to be subsumed under one name. Two regular confusions which blur its identification are to associate it with experimental music or with avant-garde music. It is true that they are very often lumped together but this is probably done for the benefit of promoters who need to know that the one thing they do have in common is a shared inability to hold the attention of large groups of casual listeners. But although they might share the same corner of the market place they are fundamentally quite different to each other. Improvisors might conduct occasional experiments but very few, I think, consider their work to be experimental. Similarly, the attitudes and precepts associated with the avant-garde have very little in common with those held by most improvisors. There are innovations made, as one would expect, through improvisation, but the desire to stay ahead of the field is not common among improvisors. And as regards method, the improvisor employs the oldest in music-making.

The lack of precision over its naming is, if anything, increased when we come to the thing itself. Diversity is its most consistent characteristic. It has no stylistic or idiomatic commitment. It has no prescribed idiomatic sound. The characteristics of freely improvised music are established only by the sonic-musical identity of the person or persons playing it.

Historically, it pre-dates any other music – mankind's first musical performance couldn't have been anything other than a free improvisation – and I think that it is a reasonable speculation that at most times since then there will have been some music-making most aptly described as free improvisation. Its accessibility to the performer is, in fact, something which appears to offend both its supporters and detractors. Free improvisation, in addition to being a highly skilled musical craft, is open to use by almost anyone – beginners, children and non-musicians. The skill and intellect required is whatever is available. It can be an activity of enormous complexity and sophistication, or the simplest and most direct expression: a lifetime's study and work or a casual dilettante activity. It can appeal to and serve the musical purposes of all kinds of people and perhaps the type of person offended by the thought that 'anyone can do it' will find some reassurance in learning that Albert Einstein looked upon improvisation as an emotional and intellectual necessity.[1]

The emergence of free improvisation as a cohesive movement in the early sixties and its subsequent continuous practice has excited a profusion of sociological, philosophical, religious and political explanations, but I shall have to leave those to authors with the appropriate appetite and ability. Perhaps I can confine myself to the obvious assumption that much of the impetus toward free improvisation came from the questioning of musical language. Or more correctly, the questioning of the 'rules' governing musical language. Firstly from the effect this had in jazz, which was the most widely practised improvised music at the time of the rise of free improvisation, and secondly from the results of the much earlier developments in musical language in European straight music, whose conventions had, until this time, exerted a quite remarkable influence over many types of music, including most forms of improvisation to be found in the West.

Two important pieces of reading concerning free improvisation are Leo Smith's book *Notes: 8 Pieces* and Cornelius Cardew's 'Towards an Ethic of Improvisation', which is from his *Treatise Handbook* (published by Peters Edition). Each of these documents is written by a musician with a great deal of experience of free improvisation and they write of it with insight and pertinence. They are however totally different from each other. Smith speaks of free improvisation almost exclusively as an extension of jazz and Cardew considers it mainly in terms of European philosophy and indeterminate composition. And both accounts are valid, each reflecting perfectly one of the twin approaches to free improvisation which took place in the sixties. It is necessary to point out that for Leo Smith the predicament of the black man in America, particularly as this applies to the black musician, is of far greater significance than the purely musical matters dealt with here. In a rather similar way Cardew's objections to his situation were later to take a purely political form. But these documents also indicate that for musicians of integrity, in either field, wishing for a direct, unadulterated involvement in music, the way to free improvisation was the obvious escape from the rigidity and formalism of their respective musical backgrounds.

---

1 Alexander Moszkowski reported that in 1919 Einstein told him '...improvisation on the piano was a necessity of his life. Every journey that takes him away from the instrument for some time excites a home-sickness for his piano, and when he returns he longingly caresses the keys to ease himself of the burden of the tone experiences that have mounted up in him, giving them utterance in improvisations.' *Conversations with Einstein*, published 1921.

Opinions about free music are plentiful and differ widely. They range from the view that free playing is the simplest thing in the world requiring no explanation, to the view that it is complicated beyond discussion. There are those for whom it is an activity requiring no instrumental skill, no musical ability and no musical knowledge or experience of any kind, and others who believe it can only be reached by employing a highly sophisticated, personal technique of virtuosic dimensions. Some are attracted to it by its possibilities for musical togetherness, others by its possibilities for individual expression. There is, as far as I know, no general view to be given. So I propose to base my account of free improvisation largely on my own playing experiences within the music. Objectivity will, I am sure, be quite beyond me, but whenever possible I shall quote other views and opinions. I should emphasise that it is not my intention to try and present an overall picture of the free music scene, nor to give a definitive account of the groups mentioned. I intend only to point to certain aspects of certain groups and situations which seem to me to illustrate some of the central tenets of free improvisation.[2]

2 Nor is it my intention to make a contribution to the increasingly frequent re-writing of the history of the beginnings of free improvisation, except perhaps to mention that my first involvement with it – which left me totally confused and alienated – was in 1957. It was a confrontation which has no musical significance in this account, but it does provide some evidence that free improvisation wasn't 'started' by anybody.

JOSEPH HOLBROOKE[1]

This group, which existed from 1963 to 1966, initially played conventional jazz and by 1965 was playing totally improvised pieces. From then on it continued to play both totally improvised and part-improvised pieces. The musicians in the group were Gavin Bryars, who was then a bass player, Tony Oxley the percussionist, and myself. The stages of our collective development from playing a standard idiomatic improvisation through to playing freely improvised music seemed at the time, and even more so in retrospect, almost imperceptible. As far as one can tell, they consisted in accepting the implications of the most logical and appropriate developments in our playing, and following where they led.

While my background as a professional 'commercial' musician employed in dance halls, night clubs, and studios meant that I was always in touch with some of the practical usages of improvisation – in fact without the ability to improvise it is very difficult to survive as a musician in the musical demi-monde where most working musicians make their living – it was the other two members of the group who provided the twin bases for the development into free improvisation.

Simplified, the position was that Oxley provided the connection and interest in what were then contemporary jazz developments – from Bill Evans through John Coltrane and Eric Dolphy to Albert Ayler – while Bryars' interest was in contemporary composers: Messiaen, Boulez, Stockhausen, Cage and their followers. This combination of interests, enthusiasms, obsessions, which of course overlapped in all directions, led logically and organically to a situation where the only way to pool our efforts and the only comprehensive expression of this confluence was through a freely improvised music.

It is important to stress that the following are *recollections* of what happened. The main distortion of this retrospective description is to greatly simplify the whole process and, most particularly, to give the development of

---

1 The group's name came from Tony Oxley although it could quite easily have come from Gavin Bryars who at that time was beginning to show what was to become a lasting interest in early 20th century English music. Joseph (sometimes Josef) Holbrooke, once described as the 'cockney Wagner', was a composer of prodigious output who, although creating something of a stir in his own lifetime has been almost totally ignored since. Investigations about him produced different dates for his birth (1875 or 1878) and different dates for his death (1958 or 1961) raising the consideration that there might be more than one Joseph Holbrooke, a speculation reinforced by the staggering amount of music published under that name. It seemed a good cover for our activities.

the music a more deliberate, more calculated, intellectual character than it actually had. In fact, in all cases it was more an emotional, or instinctive, search to find something that was logical and right, or at least appropriate, to replace the inherited things which we found stilted, moribund and formal.

Initially, we were playing fairly conventionally in a jazz manner. The improvisation was on set chord sequences, usually jazz standards, and played in time. But it seems that almost from the very beginning there was a movement to expand these boundaries. The regular metre was always under attack; systematically so when Tony Oxley evolved a method of super-imposing a different time feel over the original, creating not a poly-rhythmic effect but a non-rhythmic effect. He and Bryars practised working with this until the feeling of a regular pulse was totally removed. Additionally, harmonic experiments were taking place, an example of which is a composition of Bryars', a more or less conventional tune in 3/4 time, in which the soloist improvised not on the chord being played but on the following chord, the chord about to played. We were also following at that time certain aspects of the recorded work of Scott LaFaro and John Coltrane. All these moves constituted an attack on the harmonic and rhythmic framework within which we were working but when we did eventually break that framework it was once again only through gradual, not wholesale, moves. One of the first of these was to break the metre down. Having reached the point where the aural effect we were achieving was one of playing out of time it began to seem almost perverse not to actually play out of time. A soloist would now stay on each chord for as long as he wished to improvise on it, making the change to the next chord how and when he wished, taking his accompanists with him. Tony Oxley: 'This was rhythmically very useful to me. It was a release from the dogma of the beat.' The move away from a set harmonic sequence was to modal playing. The vehicles for this were usually either John Coltrane pieces from that period or a series of modal pieces written at that time by all three of us. We spent much time playing modally, and our earliest 'free' improvisations had a definite modal orientation.

This was probably the easiest way to start. Except, of course, that it wasn't free. It was modal. Still, it provided a base from which we could explore rhythmic and scalar relationships fairly freely. In order to escape the constant threat of the eternally suspended resolution we turned our attention to intervallic manipulation of pitch. Our influences here were partly a belated interest in Webern and partly some aspects of John Coltrane's improvisations. The main stimulus, however, was to escape from the lack of tension endemic in tonal or modal pitch constructions. The 'tension and release' myth upon which most scalar and arpeggio patterns, phrases and designs are based seemed to us no longer valid. In these closed systems there is a circular quality to the improvisation which means that the release is built into the tension, that the answer is contained in the question. The effect is of slackness, blandness. The modal setting particularly, without the restriction or discipline of an idiom, seemed to invite a facile, vacuous type of improvisation. It was to escape from this that we turned to a more atonal, non-causal organisation of the pitch. Much of our language now was arrived at by the exclusion of the elements we didn't want, which very often turned out to be mainstays of our previous tonal language, and by a much more consistent use of the more 'dissonant' intervals. There was some use of serial devices.

Bryars introduced what he describes as 'the serial equivalent of a free jazz ballad'. We each had a series of notes, with alternatives, and each note was held as long as the player wished. So there was a continuous changing harmony. There were attempts to improvise serially. Working in 3 or 4 note cells, 1 or 2 notes being held in common between successive cells. Oxley at this time started to change his instrument from a kit designed to supply set rhythmic patterns to one with an increased potential for varied sounds, timbres and percussive effects. An example of this is the occasion when, after hearing Bryars' newly acquired record of Cage's *First Constructions in Metal*, Oxley, impressed by the gong glissando effect, tried to find a way to emulate it. This he eventually did by tying a piece of cloth to a cymbal in such a way as to be able to bend the cymbal after it had been struck. It was probably years later that we discovered that the gong gliss effect was created by immersing it in water. But this was the sort of thing that was influencing the music we played. About his bass playing at this time, Bryars says: 'I very often played chords on the bass: triple stops, double stops, I always played 3 finger pizzicato, and I played horizontally across the strings like a flamenco guitarist. Ascending was usually in fast runs, descending in disjunct leaps. Scale steps going up and large steps down. But when these things became clichéd I can remember consciously trying to drop them. I would at all times try and avoid playing the pulse of the music.'

These were some of the means by which we reacted against the restrictions of the inherited improvising language, its nostalgia, and looked for fresher, less worn material with which to work. By this time most of the music was collectively improvised and solos were unaccompanied. Such accompaniment as happened was a sort of occasional commentary from the other instruments.

So the whole was somewhat atonal in character, played in a discontinuous, episodic manner, with two instruments – amplified guitar and percussion – matched to the volume of a very softly played double-bass. But the experience of playing freely soon had the effect, as it always does, of producing a set of characteristics unique to that particular grouping of musicians and of producing an identity only a small proportion of which was established by the technical, purely musical constituents.

I asked Tony Oxley, years after the events, if he could recall any particular musical landmarks in this period.

The actual technical details weren't for me the most rewarding part. It was the involvement in something that was challenging. Although the results, of course, were how we judged each stage. Sometimes there were disappointments, sometimes it was good. But the whole thing, the two or three years process, that was the important thing to me. There were times that were significant that one remembers but my main impression is one of continuous development. The search was always for something that sounded right to replace the things that sounded predictable and wrong. But there is something I would like to point out. During the whole of that time I don't think I ever made any intellectual decision to limit myself. The exclusion of the jazz vocabulary was an emotional act of feeling. Sometimes there's an assumption that this sort of thing is done just to be different. That's totally wrong. It's an emotional demand that you have to meet. When you're wearing chains you don't become aware of them through intellectual processes. You can feel them. At the time, the reasons for changing are not considered. They seem irrefutable. It is the details that you are involved with. You get on with it. There's no question about the reasons behind it. The philosophy is plain and accepted.

One of the things which was recalled was the spaciousness in the group. It was a group which seemed to offer a great deal of room or space which had a logical, appropriate feeling about it. This is difficult to come by. It is easy enough to play silence but difficult to get it to sound right.

That was the thing about the music that was most marked, particularly for percussion: the fact that silence was valid. The music started from silence. It didn't start from the rhythm section 'getting it on'. It started from what we accept as silence. And every move meant something. And for percussion that was fantastic. Because 'let's get swinging' was one of the percussionist's chains. So, to be able to make a sound and for it to mean something was a great release for me. In other terms, that contributed to the musical environment by representing, in spite of the obvious energy that was about, a respect for what the other person was doing. That was a great liberating force from the point of view of developing the necessary intense concentration on what was going on around you. One of the remarkable things about the Sheffield experience for me was that I felt that I suddenly wasn't involved with the jazz language but that I was involved in a universal language. And I feel that now. A music that carries its own judgements and intentions and is not something simply tagged on to the end of jazz. That was an enormous liberating force.

* * *

In discussing Joseph Holbrooke with Gavin Bryars I mentioned being amazed that when we first played freely it appeared to work; something I hadn't really expected. Gavin Bryars:

I think it worked for a lot of reasons. The main one was that we had gone through a period of inventing procedures together and all that stuff was insurance against things falling flat when we did work without guidelines. The fact that we did all that meant that the music retained some coherence. The earlier stuff served as a sort of training. We had been in that 'swimming' situation before, but now we moved from the shallow to the deep end. And aurally our first excursions into free playing were probably very little different from our so-called 'conventional' playing. We were already working harmonically, melodically and rhythmically in areas that were very remote from the original material. In those earlier things there was a certain energy, a certain questioning going on that was exciting.

During this period we worked every evening in a nightclub, an environment where the response to this kind of thing, although not uniformly hostile, could carry drastic sanctions. So, these developments came about mainly through private, daytime, playing and also at a weekly lunchtime concert we organised throughout that two and a half year period in a small upstairs room over a pub. During that time we collected a small audience which attended these performances with astonishing regularity and faithfulness, the bulk of them coming to the 'club' throughout its existence. Most audiences appear to prefer knowing exactly what they are going to get. Our audience couldn't have been sure of that. I asked Gavin Bryars what he thought the reasons were for their faithfulness or, perhaps, their tolerance.

There was a social aspect to the activity and there was some sort of respect – a recognition of our seriousness. It was certainly quite different from most other jazz clubs in the area. I think one reason that the audience stuck with us was that the music did have a powerful dramatic quality. There was a sense of expectancy, things did change and resolve, and so it had a kind of drama.

It was at the club that we occasionally augmented the basic trio, adding whoever might be interested to play with us. And a number of musicians were interested but as time went on the group obviously presented increasing difficulties to 'sitters in'. Gavin Bryars:

We never fully accepted other musicians into the group. They hadn't been through that period of working together and, although one welcomed their contribution, we were always vaguely suspicious that they didn't understand what was going on. We took each other seriously because of our mutual development but maybe we couldn't extend that trust to people who hadn't shared it.

Did you consider what we did to be jazz?

The earliest stuff certainly was jazz and some of the early developments followed contemporary jazz developments but after a while it became anti-jazz, and after that there was a complete ignoring of possible jazz aspects in the playing. Although it did retain a rhythmic energy and certain jazz details. But it was not a uniform texture. Things came and went. We stopped, after a while, following jazz events in America. In fact the last time I can recall any outside jazz reference was when Tony taped a Czechoslovakian group from the radio. And I didn't want to hear it. But it was the case that the only outlet for this thing we were doing was through a situation, and a music really, that was based on jazz. By about '65 though, I was barely interested in jazz at all. At that time I got the '61 Cage catalogue and I ordered things every week through the local music shop. So I was getting all those pieces and studying them and there was something strange about trying to reconcile that information with what we were doing. I had also got Cage's Silence *by this time and the ideas in that had quite a strong effect on me and at the same time I was studying composition with George Linstead. So I was actually listening to and thinking about and studying classical music far more than anything else. Messiaen at that time became a particular study of mine and I bought a lot of his scores and also the recording of* Chronocromie. *In fact there was an organ piece* L'Ascension *which I arranged for piano and bass which we played at the club.*

I remember the long bass solos where the room was absolutely silent and actually, sometimes, there wasn't much coming out of the bass either.

I would play very quiet harmonics with the bow and get the volume very low indeed. It wasn't for dramatic effect but it did produce that. Arco things were, I think, more sparse. I was not listening to other bass players then. Except LaFaro and that was for nostalgic reasons. But I had become very much involved in the instrument and I think a lot of things I did were to see what the instrument could do. It was very subjective. We spent a lot of attention, individually and collectively, on single sounds. There was a very tight concentration – almost a Zen quality – in the music. Making sure that we didn't do anything superfluous. There was nothing that could be called decoration. It wasn't austere though. In fact it could sound, I think, absolutely voluptuous. But there were times, particularly later, when we were prepared to let people be on their own for long periods. For instance we would have the

*drums playing alone for a long time but with occasional interjections from the
other instruments. And there were cadenza-like passages in the music. Solos
were usually completely solo and what accompanying there was would be
more like prompting but it wasn't a question and answer thing. It was, I think,
much more subtle than that. Even now I have a lot of respect for the music we
played and it had qualities which I haven't heard in any other improvised
music.*

*The music in terms of time was pretty expansive. Originally we might
play eight or ten pieces, probably more, in a couple of hours. When we were
playing freely we would play maybe three or four at the most. So each piece
was tending towards a half hour duration.*

Sheffield, the city in which all this was taking place, is my hometown and I
had left it some ten years before these events in search of a more stimulating
musical environment believing at the time that Sheffield represented, in its
musical life, all the deadliest aspects of provincialism. Now, having returned
for reasons unconnected with music, there was a certain irony in stumbling
into such a fertile musical situation. The transformation was, of course, more
to do with people than place but Gavin pointed to the advantages of isolation
for what we were doing.

*I think the fact that we were isolated, musically, helped us. Normally I'm
suspicious of that idea, particularly the idea of composers in isolation, but I
think for us it made a lot of difference. Had we been playing in London, say,
some area with a large musical community, most of the developments would
have been nipped in the bud. Over two and a half years there was constant
contact between us and, as far as our creative musical activities were
concerned, we only worked with each other. In London or some other centre
there would have been other interests and influences. We developed a
collective language. Not a consciously articulated language but step by step –
each step by a different person – a symbiotic thing. The total exceeded the sum
of the individual parts. It was a very real case of that. It was absolutely a
collective thing. The ideas that were contributed individually all coloured the
development but we were in a position to trust each other sufficiently to share
those things, to allow the individual contributions to come in and be used
collectively.*

Amongst the many things enjoyed by that group was the productive
contrast between the musical personalities of Gavin Bryars and Tony Oxley.
Bryars had a somewhat ambivalent attitude toward the group then, never sure
if he should be there at all, but knowing, I think, that it suited his musical
position at that time (he subsequently became a composer). Combined as it
was with a certain natural anarchic tendency it contrasted sharply with

92

Oxley's direct, totally committed stance. This kind of juxtaposition has the effect of producing a continuous, slight, musical friction which is, I think, very productive in an improvising group. But that was only one among a host of benefits which flowed from being able to work so closely with two, quite differently, exceptional musicians and which made being a part of Joseph Holbrooke an incomparable musical experience for me.

THE MUSIC IMPROVISATION COMPANY

From shortly after its formation in 1968 to its disintegration in 1971 the Music Improvisation Company was Evan Parker, saxophones; Hugh Davies, live electronics; Jamie Muir, percussion; and myself, guitar. For the last year or so of its existence Christine Jeffrey was in the group. Her role was usually described as voice which, although inadequate, was probably the only possible description of her extraordinary sonic abilities.

The live electronics were introduced into the group as a further extension of the alienation, in materials and sounds, from idiomatic improvisation; a continuation of the search for a style-less, uncommitted area in which to work. As Evan Parker says:

We were looking to extend the range of timbres available and to balance the overt virtuosity that was central to our instrumental approach at the time with another type of playing approach. We wanted some sounds which weren't associated with instrumental improvisation.

In practice it wasn't always like that. After an initial period of adjustment the live electronics developed a more conventional instrumental presence, in some respects, than the other 'normal' instruments. His adoption of the amplified long string, for instance, resulted in Davies often producing the sort of electric guitar open string sound that I was at pains to avoid. There was often a greater variety of timbre to be found in the saxophone than in the live electronics. The few tonal references found in the music were usually produced by the same source. So instead of the anticipated result, the live electronics served to extend the music both forwards and backwards, so to speak, and Davies helped to loosen what had been, until his arrival, a perhaps too rarefied approach. Altogether it was a good example of a musician creating a role from his own musical perceptions, not allowing it to be dictated solely by the 'nature' of his instrument or the expectations of his colleagues. Evan Parker points to other aspects of Davies' contribution.

Hugh's virtuosity was expressed more in the building of an instrument than in the playing. Playing most of his instruments was often a matter of letting them speak, but at the right time and at the right dynamic level. His work with the group also hastened the development of the several 'layers' approach to improvising, extending the basic dialogue form of the music which has been called ping-pong.

Davies' own view of the MIC, as expressed in an issue of *Musics Magazine*, is:

> *...you could play in the secure knowledge that one or more of the other players, almost always particular players that one was 'aiming at', would react to you in a particular way, without necessarily playing the sort of thing that you might have expected them to play – in other words a security which enabled unrestricted exploration of the new musical possibilities to take place.*

When I indicated to Hugh Davies that it surprised me that the Music Improvisation Company gave anyone a feeling of security he gave the following example of what he meant.

> *The most specific memory – indeed virtually the only one – that I have of a particular 'incident' during one of the performances of the Music Improvisation Company, is of a concert that we gave in Durham. At one point Evan Parker began to play extremely high notes on his soprano saxophone, fairly fast figuration within a small pitch-range, very intense and clearly quite an effort to maintain. I knew that he was expecting another musician to join him up there – musically speaking it was almost as if he was asking one of us to do so – and at that moment I was not only perhaps the most obvious choice because of the suitability of my instruments, but also I was not playing at the time and thus was free to join him. However, I waited until he had very nearly given up for lack of response, before suddenly taking up his invitation, which meant that he then had to continue, for longer than he had 'intended' when he started out; musically it would have been virtually impossible for him to desert me immediately, as it would have destroyed the logic of what he had just been playing (possibly, even if he actually remembered this situation, Evan would disagree about this!). I took this decision for purely musical reasons, without verbally rationalising it for myself, as it created a musical tension that developed out of Evan's initial gesture that seemed to me to be appropriate. Of course it was also typical of the way in which we functioned as a group, both musically and on the level of personal interaction (which are virtually identical, and certainly inseparable). Had my action been on a verbal level, it could have been interpreted by an observer as being rather cruel, but it was more in the nature of teasing and at the same time intended to create a mutually stimulating musical tension. This is only possible when improvising musicians know each other well enough for a common language to have come into being, and a mutual trust in each other permits one to push against the limitations of that language and the relationships on which it is based.*

Here Hugh Davies is pointing to a feature of some free improvisation which might be described as mutual subversion. Some improvisors find this feature unhelpful, others thrive on it. But the MIC contained it to an unusually large degree.

Perhaps a clearer idea of the different forces at work in the group can be gained from the views of Jamie Muir. In an issue of the now defunct magazine *Microphone* he gave the following account of his musical philosophy.

Well let me put it another way – I much prefer junk shops to antique shops. There's nothing to find in an antique shop – it's all been found already; whereas in a junk shop it's only been collected. But a rubbish dump – a rubbish dump has been neither found nor collected – in fact it's been completely rejected – and that is the undiscovered/unidentified/unclaimed/unexplored territory – the future if only you can see it. Now some, like Yamashta, would take a rubbish dump and turn it into an antique shop – that's real alchemy, but it smacks of the gold rush and a kind of greed – of 'staking out a claim', taking from the earth but never putting back (who throws away antiques?) – he civilises vast hunks of unexplored territory and builds safari clubs all over it so you can view the beauties of the wilderness in luxurious comfort and from a safe distance – a remarkable feat but you're back safe and sound in the antique shop again where everything, you can bet your life, has already been found...and will be catalogued. However there is an alternative.

Instead of transmuting rubbish into music with a heavily predetermined qualitative bias...leave behind the biases and structures of selectivity (which is an enormous task), the 'found' attitudes you inherit, and approach the rubbish with a total respect for its nature as rubbish – the undiscovered/unidentified/unclaimed – transmuting that nature into the performing dimension. The way to discover the undiscovered in performing terms is to immediately reject all situations as you identify them (the cloud of unknowing) – which is to give music a future.

It was to this compound of attitudes and philosophies that Christine Jeffrey added her contribution, which Evan Parker describes thus:

Christine's effect was through a combination of trance and whimsy, peculiarly her own at that time. To incorporate her range of expression required that we broaden the emotional continuum of the music considerably.

The sound of the group, its whole character in fact, would depend on who was 'leader' at the time. Who was leader wasn't a matter for discussion or democratic decision. It depended on whichever member's influence, extended through psychological alliances and conspiracies, was predominant at the time. One member's leadership or dominance could have any lifespan but usually seemed to last about three or four months. During this time the group would reflect, not always without a struggle, his preferences and performing style until, exhausted by his responsibilities, the leader would be overthrown and returned to the rebellious ranks. Or that is how it seemed to me. But strangely, the overall result of the apparently contradictory forces and attitudes at work in the group was the achievement of a consistent, almost 'tight' group feeling, regardless of its changes in identity.

The bulk of the music played, as with the great majority of free improvisation, is best described, I believe, as instrumental improvisation. Instrumental as defined by Curt Sachs, writing in *The Wellsprings of Music*. 'The original concepts of vocal and of instrumental music are utterly different. The instrumental impulse is not melody in a 'melodious' sense, but an agile movement of the hands which seems to be under the control of a brain centre totally different from that which inspires vocal melody. Altogether, instrumental music, with the exception of rudimentary rhythmic percussion, is as a rule a florid, fast and brilliant display of virtuosity... Quick motion is not merely a means to a musical end but almost an end in itself which always connects with the fingers, the wrists and the whole of the body.' That would serve as a description of one of the underlying forces in free improvisation.

It is the attitude of the player to this tactile element, to the physical experience of playing an instrument, to the 'instrumental impulse' which establishes much of the way he plays. One of the basic characteristics of his improvising, detectable in everything he plays, will be how he harnesses the instrumental impulse. Or how he reacts against it. And this makes the stimulus and the recipient of this impulse, the instrument, the most important of his musical resources.

THE MIC – THE INSTRUMENT

In the non-improvisor, particularly the straight player, there is no sign of the instrumental impulse. One reason why the standard Western instrumental training produces non-improvisors (and it doesn't just produce violinists, pianists, cellists, etcetera: it produces specifically non-improvisors, musicians rendered incapable of attempting improvisation) is that not only does it teach how to play an instrument, it teaches that the creation of music is a separate activity from playing that instrument. Learning how to create music is a separate study totally divorced from playing an instrument. Music for the instrumentalist is a set of written symbols which he interprets as best he can. They, the symbols, are the music, and the man who wrote them, the composer, is the music-maker. The instrument is the medium through which the composer finally transmits his ideas. The instrumentalist is not required to make music. He can assist with his 'interpretation' perhaps, but, judging from most reported remarks on the subject, composers prefer the instrumentalist to limit his contribution to providing the instrument, keeping it in tune and being able to use it to carry out, as accurately as possible, any instructions which might be given to him. The improvisor's view of the instrument is totally different.

About learning to play an instrument John Stevens says: 'Improvisation is the basis of learning to play a musical instrument. But what usually happens? You decide you want a certain instrument. You buy the instrument and then think to yourself, "I'll go and find a teacher, and who knows, in seven or eight years' time I might be able to play this thing". And in that way you miss a mass of important musical experience. Studying formally with a teacher might be the right way to achieve certain specific aims, but to do only that is a very distorted way of approaching a musical instrument. It has to be realised that a person's own investigation of an instrument – his exploration of it – is totally valid.'

* * *

There seem to be two main attitudes to the instrument among improvisors. One is that the instrument is man's best friend, both a tool and a helper; a collaborator. The other attitude is that the instrument is unnecessary, at worst

98

a liability, intruding between the player and his music. The division between these views is not as distinct as it might seem, but the first, the pro-instrument view, is the most widely held and is found in all areas of improvisation. With the instrument, as with other things, attitudes and practices found in 'conventional' forms of improvisation can be found, sometimes developed and extended, in free improvisation; but the instrument, in free playing, can assume an absolutely central position, a position to which its historic functions might be quite irrelevant. Steve Lacy: 'The instrument – that's the matter – the stuff – your subject.'

There is no generalised technique for playing any musical instrument. However one learns to play an instrument it is always for a specific task. The Indian player, after successful study with his master, is fitted to play Indian music. The flamenco player learns flamenco, the jazz player jazz, and so on. And in some respects the better he is at his chosen idiom the more specialised his abilities become.

The standard European instrumental education thinks of itself as being an exception to this rule. It is of course a very good example of it. It equips a musician with the ability to perform the standard European repertoire and its derivatives, and perhaps more than any other discipline it limits its adherents' ability to perform in other musical areas.

Although some improvisors employ a high level of technical skill in their playing, to speak of 'mastering' the instrument in improvisation is misleading. The instrument is not just a tool but an ally. It is not only a means to an end, it is a source of material, and technique for the improvisor is often an exploitation of the natural resources of the instrument. He might develop certain aspects of the instrument that appeal to him, that seem particularly fruitful. The unorthodox technique is commonplace, its function being to serve only one man's purpose: 'technique for the improvisor is not an arbitrary consumption of an abstract standardised method but rather a direct attunement with the mental, spiritual and mechanical energy necessary to express a full creative impulse' (Leo Smith)[1].

Probably a large part of most improvising techniques is developed to meet particular situations encountered in performance. But most practical musical situations imply other hypothetical situations, and so one technical device might be developed to cover a wide range of possibilities. An extension of technique might have certain musical implications which might in turn

---

1 John Stevens speaks of something similar to this. 'Around the time we made *Karyobin*, I thought "there's my arms, there's my legs, and there is enough flexibility there for anything". All I had to find was a way of applying myself. And I didn't want to dabble with that flexibility. I didn't want to practise or anything. So I went through that period and at that time it worked. Now it's different. I like to play the drums all the time. But for that time it worked. And I still believe in it. Application is even more important than technical facility, because application is the key to taking part, to being involved.'

produce further technical implications, which might reveal further musical implications – that sort of extrapolation or rationalisation is one of the many ways in which the instrument can supply the music. Almost any aspect of playing an instrument can reveal music. Virtuosity doesn't have to be empty, however irresistible that phrase might be for the critic. The instrument's responsiveness to its acoustic environment, how it reacts to other instruments and how it reacts to the physical aspects of performing, can vary enormously. The accidental can be exploited through the amount of control exercised over the instrument, from complete – producing exactly what the player dictates – to none at all – letting the instrument have its say. Habits – technical habits and musical habits (clichés) – are quite consciously utilised by some performers. And there is a type of creative impetus which can come from playing well technically which can't be achieved in any other way. There also seem to be direct technical benefits from a concentration on the creative, not on the executive, side of playing.

In addition to developing a personal instrumental technique it is common amongst pro-instrument improvisors to develop, and literally to extend, their instruments. Some of these changes can be quite minimal; a loose string added to a guitar, altered mutes and mouthpieces for a trombone, the usual sort of 'preparations' for a piano. More radically, extension is made by amplification and electronic treatment. Although this is mainly confined to string players, many improvisors are attracted to the use of electronics and it is one of the many kinds of instrument extension to be found amongst percussion players.

Any object at all can be included in an improvising percussionist's equipment. The usual basic stuff – drums, cymbals, wood blocks, xylophones, etcetera – is supplemented by gongs, saucepans, gunshells, handbells and all the other early-Cage paraphernalia. There are also devices used which would probably find their antecedents in the armoury of futurist composer Luigi Russolo, who used to describe his noise-makers as 'howlers, roarers, cracklers, whistlers, rubbers, buzzers, exploders, gurglers and rustlers'.

The percussionist Frank Perry, describing his kit, writes: 'superimposed about these [drums and cymbals] are a variety of sound sources. These comprise small bells, wood blocks, cowbells – chimes, hubcaps. The various things hanging include: knives and forks, stones, plastic spoons, sea shells, brass fittings and bamboo. Wire knitting needles, chopsticks and other strikers obviously extend these characteristics.'[2]

---

2 This quotation is taken from the June 1972 issue of the magazine *Microphone*, unfortunately defunct. This issue of the magazine, from which I have already taken some remarks of Jamie Muir's, was given over to the views and comments of improvising percussionists. In the same issue, Paul Lytton said 'the sources have remained the same: wood, plastic, metal, wire, rubber, skin, liquid, gas'.

Quite differently, Tony Oxley's percussion equipment, although including many acoustic items, leans more to electronic extension. The acoustic part is: drums – eight, various sizes and textures; cymbals – fourteen, various sizes, thicknesses, weights, sounds; cowbells – five, from 6 inches to 16 inches; wood surfaces – five, wood blocks and oriental skulls; saucepans – two. The amplified section of the kit is: amplified frame containing cymbals, wires, various kitchen equipment, motor generators, springs, used with 3 contact mikes (home-made), 2 volume pedals, 1 octave splitter, 1 compressor, 1 ring modulator and oscillator, 1 amplifier and 2 speakers.

Since the heyday of the mammoth percussion kit, when they were measured in the number of hours needed to erect and dismantle them, there has been a definite tendency towards more modest constructions, and the contrast between the pro- and anti- instrument view, amongst percussion players at least, is not now so vivid.

* * *

The anti-instrument attitude might be presented as: 'The instrument comes between the player and his music.' 'It doesn't matter what sort of instrument you play, a Stradivarius or a tin drum, it's the person behind it that counts.' Technically, the instrument has to be defeated. The aim is to do on the instrument what you could do if you could play without an instrument. Ronnie Scott expressed this view when he said: 'I practise to become as close to the instrument, as familiar with it, as possible. The ideal thing would be to be able to play the instrument as one would play a kazoo.' And in conventional or traditional improvising it does usually mean the musician would like to be in such complete control that the instrument ceases to be a consideration. In free improvisation where one's intentions do not necessarily have a prescribed aural definition, this attitude can lead to a rejection of the instrument entirely and the utilisation of other sonic resources, usually accompanied by an increase in theatrical activity. More usually, though, the second attitude leads to a limiting of technique and a reduction of the instrument to its 'essentials'. Again percussion players provide the best examples: one plays a three piece toy drum set; another plays only a military snare drum. Most of the musicians in this grouping share an almost pathological hatred of anything which might be called electronic.

Instruments very much in favour with this school are, naturally enough, those which are ethnic in origin or, at least, in appearance. These meet the requirement that the instrument should have a fixed, very limited capability and that very little instrumental skill is needed to play it. The idea is, I think, that because of the limited opportunities for technical virtuosity, a more direct expressiveness is possible. Some of these players have shown a great interest in the practices and rituals of ethnic music and particularly in what is taken to be primitive uses of the voice. So, in performance, grunts, howls, screams, groans, Tibetan humming, Tunisian chanting, Maori chirping and Mozambique stuttering are combined with the African thumb piano, Chinese temple blocks, Ghanian soft trumpet, Trinidadian steel drum, Scottish soft bagpipe, Australian bull-roarer, Ukrainian stone flute and the Canton one-legged monster to provide an aural event about as far removed from the directness and dignity of ethnic music as a thermo-nuclear explosion is from a fart.

At one time or another, most players investigate both the pro- and the anti-instrument approaches, some oscillate continuously between them and some contrive to hold both views at once, so there is no clear division into two groups of musicians. But the attitudes are quite distinct, it seems to me, and both can be heard in almost any piece of improvised music.

THE MIC – RECORDING

My songs are part of my soul and if the demon in the white man's box steals my soul, why, I must die. Eskimo refusing to record for ethnomusicologist.

Describing a musical event as a "free improvisation", recording it and issuing it for people to listen to in their front rooms lays a philosophical and aesthetic minefield. From a review by Michael Thorne of *Free Improvisation* (Deutsche Grammophon, 3-box set).

The Music Improvisation Company made two records: the one on the Incus label provides the best example of the group's recording style and establishes the identity of the group at that period (1969-70). But in common with other recordings of free improvisation – possibly any improvisation – what it does not do is present a piece of the group's music. Too little of improvised music survives recording. One of the reasons is quite simple. The technical illusions practised in recording ('live' or studio) are inimical to the constantly changing balances and roles which operate within most free improvisation. Recording devices such as reduction, 'presence', compression limiting, filtering and stereo picture, usually serve only to fillet out or disturb quite important elements.

But much more important than the limitations of the technology is the loss during the recording process of the atmosphere of musical activity – the musical environment created by the performance – 'the matching of music with place and occasion', as Peter Riley describes it, which is one of the main strengths of improvisation. Ronnie Scott says: 'I hate making records, I really detest making records, because to me the way I play is really a kind of momentary thing, an in-person momentary thing, that one can't hope to capture on a record, simply because it is a record.' Cornelius Cardew, discussing the recording of free improvisation, says: 'What recording produces is a separate phenomenon, something really much stranger than the playing itself, since what you hear on tape or disc is indeed the same playing but divorced from its natural context. What is the importance of the natural context? The natural context provides a score which the players are unconsciously interpreting – a score that co-exists inseparably with the music, standing side by side with it and sustaining it.' Lionel Salter on recording baroque music: 'I'm not at all sure that recording is useful for anything more than reference.' Alain Danielou: 'Of the living music in which improvisation plays an essential part, a gramophone record gives us only a frozen or fixed moment, like a photograph of a dancer.' All that a recording can offer are certain identifiable features. Features which, although completely unique and personal to that group or individual, are useful only for purposes of identification. That it should provide evidence of musical identity or of changes in identity is all that is usually claimed for a recording.

The intermittent fuss over the validity of recording improvisation overlooks certain realities. Recording is an adjunct to all musical activities except those which exist as an adjunct to recording. Many of the reservations expressed about recorded improvisation apply equally well to other recorded music. Records simply supply a different listening experience to listening 'live'; for the majority of people, apparently, a preferable one. Perhaps the debate over recording improvised music keeps rearing its head because, unlike other recorded music, there is no apparent economic justification for it.

* * *

Compared to some groups, the Music Improvisation Company had a relatively short life span. After less than three years, and after a particularly fruitful late period, it came apart. Evan Parker, referring to the last twelve months of the group's existence, says:

Being part of the group through this period opened me to the point where, when the wind's in the right direction, I'm ready to play with anyone. The last few occasions the M.I.C. played remain sharply etched in my memory and are amongst my most highly valued playing experiences.

SOLO

Improvisors are, as a rule, musically gregarious, preferring to work with other musicians in any combination from duo up to quite inexplicably large ensembles. For most people improvisation, although a vehicle for self expression, is about playing with other people and some of the greatest opportunities provided by free improvisation are in the exploration of relationships between players. In this respect solo improvisation makes no sense at all. However, at some time or other, most improvisors investigate the possibility of playing solo. Historically, the earliest documentation of improvisation, almost the only documentation of improvisation, concerns solo playing. Much of this deals with the organ, but there are also accounts describing the popularity of solo improvising on all the string and keyboard instruments. Solo improvising, in fact, attained a quite exceptional pre-eminence in Europe during the 17th century when great facility in this art was considered, apparently, to be a sign of good breeding. Curiously, in our own time, never outdone in hyperbole, the efforts of an improvisor to make sense of the solo situation have been described as noble.

My conversations with other improvisors on the topic of solo playing produced a variety of opinions, to which I will return, but no general view emerged that I could detect so again I'll attempt, without too much optimism, to describe what I think is my own approach to solo playing. This, I find, has changed considerably as time has gone on. Much of what I assumed about my own solo playing when I first tried to write about it fifteen years ago no longer seems particularly relevant to what I think I do now. The implications of this for the permanence of my present assumptions will be obvious.

For me there has always been an attraction in solo playing, perhaps partly explained by the nature and tradition of the guitar, the instrument I play. But when, around 1970/71 after a period of some years playing in improvising groups of many different styles and sizes, I turned almost exclusively to solo improvising, I did so out of necessity. The need, after a considerable time thinking only in group terms, was to have a look at my own playing and to find out what was wrong with it and what was not wrong with it. I wanted to know if the language I was using was complete, if it could supply everything that I wanted in a musical performance. The ideal way of doing this, perhaps the only way, it seemed to me, was through a period of solo playing. Alternating periods of group playing with solo playing is something I have tried to maintain ever since.

The analogy with language, often used by improvising musicians in discussing their work, has a certain usefulness in illustrating the development of a common stock of material – a vocabulary – which takes place when a group of musicians improvise together regularly. With a successful improvising group the bulk of their material will be initially provided by the styles, techniques and habits of the musicians involved. This vocabulary will then be developed by the musicians individually, in work and research away from the group, and collectively, in performance. In a wider sense, Steve Lacy speaks of a 'brotherhood of language. Each player who comes along affects the common pool of language. When you hear a new player – and you make it your business to hear anyone who comes along who has something new – then you have to go back and rethink everything.'

In the choice and development of material the solo improvisor works in similar ways to the group improvisor. Building a personal vocabulary and working to extend it in both performance and preparation. The material is never fixed and its historical and systematic associations can be ignored. The improvisor can also look for material which will be appropriate for, and which will facilitate, improvisation. This last consideration, for me, provides the main purpose and the continuing interest in solo playing. It forms part of the search for whatever is endlessly variable, the construction of a language, all parts of which are always and equally available.

The most obvious differences to group improvisation – greater cohesiveness and easier control for the soloist – are not, in improvisation, necessarily advantages and an even greater loss, of course, is the unpredictable element usually provided by other players. In this situation the language becomes much more important and there will be times in solo improvisation when the player relies entirely on the vocabulary used. At such times, when other more aesthetically acceptable resources such as invention and imagination have gone missing, the vocabulary becomes the sole means of support. It has to provide everything needed to sustain continuity and impetus in the musical performance. This, it seems to me, is where the main danger in solo improvisation arises.

Improvising alone, before an audience, is not without its terrors. The temptation, when nothing else seems to be offering itself, to resort to tried and proven procedures, to flog those parts of the performance which are most palatable to an audience – and no musician who has spent time playing in

106

public is in any doubt about what they are – is not easily resisted and it is clear that in solo improvising, as with a great deal of performed music, a successful audience response can be the cause of rituals and formulae being repeatedly trotted out long after they have lost any musical motivation. At this point the credibility of the activity is in the balance and maintaining it simply depends on the courage of the player. Once solo playing descends to being the recycling of previously successful formulae its relevance to improvisation becomes pretty remote.

* * *

The developments in my playing following on from those described in the chapter on Joseph Holbrooke continued along the same lines and for the same reasons: to find a way of dealing with a freely improvised situation in which a conventional vocabulary proved inadequate. Again, a written description – any description – is, inevitably, a distortion, ossifying and delineating a process which was fluid and amorphous – and almost always empirical.

Beyond the immediate influence of the musicians I was playing with, the bases of my improvising language came from an interest in the music of Schoenberg's pre-serial, 'free' atonal period, the later music of Webern and also certain early electronic music composers. (Musicians who shared, it is fairly safe to say, a deep antipathy to anything remotely connected with improvisation.) Apart from the fact that I liked the stuff, I thought (and I still think) that intervallic manipulation of pitch is less restricting and more productive than other ways of pitch management, and that the very clearly differentiated changes of timbre which characterised some early electronic music was the sort of thing which could assist in assembling a language that would be literally disjointed, whose constituents would be unconnected in any causal or grammatical way and so would be more open to manipulation. A language based on malleable, not pre-fabricated, material. Generally I was looking, I think, to utilise those elements which stem from the concepts of unpredictability and discontinuity, of perpetual variation and renewal first introduced into European composition at the beginning of the 20th century.

But this 'improvising language' was, of course, superimposed upon another musical language; one learned, also empirically, over many years as a working musician. Working musicians, those found earning a living in night clubs, recording studios, dance halls and any other place where music has a functional role, spend very little time, as I remember it, discussing 'improvising language', but anyone lacking the ability to invent something, to add something, to *improve* something would quickly prove to be in the wrong business. In that world, improvisation is a fact of musical life. And it seems to me that this bedrock of experience, culled in a variety of situations, occasionally bubbles up in one way or another, particularly playing solo. Not affecting specifics like pitch or timbre or rhythmic formulations (I've yet to find any advantage in quoting directly any of the kinds of music I used to play) but influencing decisions that affect overall balance and pace – judging what will work. The unexpected, not to say the unnerving, can also occasionally appear. Recently, it seems to me, some reflection of the earliest guitar music I ever heard occasionally surfaces in my solo playing; music I have had no connection with, either as listener or player, since childhood.

Once a vocabulary of some homogeneity is assembled and is working and has proved to be usable in a playing situation, material can be included, at least for a period, from any source. And that's a necessity, because the need for material is endless. A feeling of freshness is essential and the best way to get that is for some of the material to be fresh. In a sense it is change for the sake of change. Change for the sake of the benefits that change can bring.

Eventually, the attempt to analyse one's playing in this way reveals, among other things, the limitations of the vocabulary/language analogy. The flute player Jim Denley points out the automatic simplification that occurs whatever kind of explanation is attempted:

> For the improvisor the physicality of producing sound (the hardware) is not a separate activity to the thoughts and ideas in music (software). In the act of creation there is a constant loop between the hierarchy of factors involved in the process. My lungs, lips, fingers, voice box and their working together with the potentials of sound are dialoguing with other levels which I might call mind and perception. The thoughts and decisions are sustained and modified by my physical potentials and vice versa but as soon as I try and define these separately I run into problems. It is a meaningless enterprise for it is the very entanglement of levels of perception, awareness and physicality that makes improvisation.[1]

* * *

Talking with other improvisors about solo playing revealed that most people see it as a vehicle for self-expression. A way of presenting a personal music. One curious uniformity of attitude, or at least explanation, was the use of Paul Klee's 'Taking a line for a walk'. Evan Parker, Christine Jeffrey and Phil Wachsmann have all quoted it at different times in talking about what they do.

---

1 From 'Improvisation: the entanglement of awareness and physicality', a paper by Jim Denley published in the improvisation issue (Summer 1991) of *Sounds Australian*.

Leo Smith says: '...one improvisor creates a complete improvisation with more than one instrument and of mixed character (eg trumpet, flugelhorn, percussion instruments and flute.)' And then the opposite approach is suggested by Tony Oxley: 'In solo playing at the moment I'm limiting myself to certain aspects of the kit, just a part of the vocabulary. I find that an interesting thing. It's obviously more secure than the wide open thing.'

It is clear that in solo playing the instrument achieves a special potency and its importance to this kind of music-making is at its most obvious here. In some cases, the music is literally constructed from the instrument, as with instrument builders such as Hugh Davies and Max Eastley. The German guitar player Hans Reichal, who seems to have spent the greater part of his career playing solo, has built a series of guitars of unique design, each modification reflected in the music he plays on them. For others, special instrumental techniques form the basis of their approach.

Solo playing, in fact, has produced some remarkable, even spectacular, performances, usually of a dense, furiously active nature: a panic of loneliness; a manic dialogue with the phantom other; virtuosic distortions of natural bodily functions unequalled since the days of La Petomaine. Missing, is the kind of playing which produces music independent of the characteristics of instruments or even individual styles ('...who played that?...'), unidentifiable passages which are the kind of magic only possible, perhaps, in group playing.

The most interesting soloists to my ears often turn out to be trombonists. Paul Rutherford and George Lewis, in their different ways, both seem to make improvisation the basis of their solo playing and also take advantage of the 'singleness' of the solo situation; happy for the music to sound like one person, playing alone. Vinko Globokar, on the other hand, the trombone player who initiated much of the vocabulary widely used by improvising trombonists (contentious area this), dismisses solo improvising as meaningless.

PRACTISING

Paco Peña: *I prepare to be able, technically, to reach anything I want to reach on the guitar and for that, of course, I do my exercises and so on. But not specifically for improvising.*

Evan Parker: *It seems to me the only practising of improvisation you could do is either to improvise or to think about improvising.*

Ronnie Scott: *I've done what for me is a great deal of practising and then played in public and my technique feels worse than it's ever been before, whereas, one can not touch the instrument for weeks, and go out and be free and loose.*

There is almost unanimity here. But concerning improvising at the organ Jean Langlais says: 'We have a technique for practising improvisation' (page 38).

With group improvisation the logic of not rehearsing is obvious, although a number of groups have examined the possibility of a kind of preparation for improvisation. Cardew says: '[there is] the proposition that improvisation cannot be rehearsed. Training is substituted for rehearsal, and a certain moral discipline is an essential part of this training.'

But with solo improvisation, as Jean Langlais indicates, there are definite possibilities for practise. Not a pre-fixing of material nor preparing devices but something which deals with and, hopefully, can be expected to improve the ability to improvise.

The practise I do divides into three areas. Firstly, the normal basic technical practise, the musical equivalent of running on the spot, the sort of thing which might be useful to the player of any music. The benefit that this sort of thing has for improvisation is debatable. Perhaps I do it because I actually like practising, but it does assist in keeping instrumentally fit, which is a playing condition that I would have thought was fairly important to an improvisor. The second area of practise is centred on exercises worked out to deal specifically with the manipulative demands made by new material. These have a bearing on the material being used and if that changes they also have to change. The third area, and I suspect this type of practise is done by many improvisors, if they practise at all, is similar to something known in jazz circles at one time as 'woodshedding'. (Do jazz players not do this now or do they call it something else?) It is the bridge between technical practise and improvisation. As personal as improvisation itself, it approximates to it but is really quite different.

Aurally this difference might manifest itself in a greater deliberateness, occasional stops and starts, and perhaps repetitions for obvious technical reasons. Or the difference between the two might not be aurally apparent at all. But it will be there and it lies in the improvisor's relationship to what he is playing. He listens to himself in a different way. He might be much more analytical and much less involved in aspects of playing created by the impetus or the tension of performance. The playing might be much the same as when improvising but the focus of attention will be on the details of playing rather than on the totality, and what is being exercised is choice.

This is the way in which I work, and I can imagine that to some improvisors it all adds up to heresy. They might subscribe to an approach which prefers an abrupt confrontation with whatever is offered by each performing situation. A self-contained unique experience undiluted by anything in the nature of preparatory musical press-ups or carefully stored ammunition. The aesthetic is faultless and perhaps leads to the ultimate ideal of improvising once and never again. Which is another reason why I favour the other, the practising, approach. The continuity of involvement which is available in solo improvisation is, for me, its main reward.

FORM

Perhaps I have given the impression that there is no forward planning, no overall structure, no 'form'. Adverse criticism of free improvisation – pretty nearly the only kind available – almost always aims itself at the same two or three targets and the clear favourite of these is 'formlessness'. As the criteria for assessing a piece of music, any piece of music, is usually inherited from the attitudes and prejudices handed down by the mandarins of European straight music this is to be expected. Nowhere is the concept of form as an ideal set of proportions which transcend style and language clung to with such terrified tenacity as by the advocates of musical composition. 'The necessity for design and balance is nowhere more imperative than in music, where all is so fleeting and impalpable – mere vibrations of the tympanic membrane.' Although written many years ago, that is still probably a fairly accurate indication of the importance attached to form by those people concerned with composed music. Even in those parts of contemporary composition where the earlier types of overall organisation no longer serve, a great deal of ingenuity is exercised in finding something upon which the music can be 'based'. Myths, poems, political statements, ancient rituals, paintings, mathematical systems; it seems that any overall pattern must be imposed to save music from its endemic formlessness.

There is no technical reason why the improvisor, particularly the solo improvisor, should not do the same thing. Most musical form is simple, not to say simple-minded. But generally speaking, improvisors don't avail themselves of the many 'frameworks' on offer. They seem to prefer formlessness. More accurately, they prefer the music to dictate its own form.

In practice, this works in many ways and, as the subconscious aim is probably to invent a form unique to every performance, giving a precise account of the complex forces that govern the shape and direction of an improvisation, even if such a thing is possible, would have no general significance. But there is a forward-looking imagination which, while mainly concerned with the moment, will prepare for later possibilities. Rather in the way that memory works, perhaps, a piece can be criss-crossed with connections and correspondences which govern the selection and re-selection of events as well as guiding the over-all pacing of the piece. Simultaneously, events remembered and events anticipated can act on the present moment. As Evan Parker says: 'Improvisation makes its own form'; and similarly, Carl T. Whitmer: 'In expansion the form is generated.' Frank Perry, the percussionist: 'For me, improvisation has meant the freeing of form that it may more readily accommodate my imagination.'

* * *

The need to isolate and examine the problems of language, to connect and to extend it, are adequately answered by solo playing. But solo playing for the improvisor can be more than that and above all can offer a method by which one can work continuously on all aspects of a body of music; an uninterrupted activity which relies not on time and place or structured opportunities for its occasion or on any of the different levels of acceptance and approval upon which performed music usually depends for its viability, but relies only on the player's ability to develop his music, to maintain its evolution, and so guarantee his own continuing involvement.

Maintaining solo playing which remains meaningful from an improvising point of view is an elusive business, not least because the easier it becomes to play solo the harder it becomes to improvise solo, but it provides many rewards and is, at times, essential.

But ultimately the greatest rewards in free improvisation are to be gained in playing with other people. Whatever the advantages to solo playing there is a whole side to improvisation; the more exciting, the more magical side, which can only be discovered by people playing together. The essence of improvisation, its intuitive, telepathic foundation, is best explored in a group situation. And the possible musical dimensions of group playing far outstrip those of solo playing.

Paradoxically, perhaps, I have found that the best base from which to approach group playing is that of being a solo improvisor. Having no group loyalties to offend and having solo playing as an ultimate resource, it is possible to play with other musicians, of whatever persuasion, as often as one wishes without having to enter into a permanent commitment to any stylistic or aesthetic position. This might be, I think, the ideal situation for an improvisor.

PART 6

OBJECTIONS

Perhaps this is a good point at which to acknowledge that the world is not divided into improvisors, those who can, and non-improvisors, those who cannot. There are, of course, musicians who can improvise, who have considerable experience of improvisation, and who have found it, for various reasons, unacceptable to them. What follows is a transcription of a conversation between Gavin Bryars and myself in which he describes his disenchantment with improvisation. I think it also indicates one of the main differences between a composer's and an improvisor's attitude towards making music.

I decided to stop working as a practicing musician, to give up the playing job I was doing and go into teaching. For some time before that I had been getting more and more interested in theoretical aspects of music. I had been reading Cage and had been involving myself more in questions of aesthetics and composition. This was the general background. But I can point to certain specific occasions which I can now recognise as being significant in my turning from improvisation.

One of them was the last time Joseph Holbrooke played together. There had been quite a long gap, maybe months, since we had worked together and because of the demands of teaching I had not spent very much time practising the bass. When we played together regularly I was always playing, but on this occasion I think I had lost touch with the instrument a bit. And the fact that I was called upon to play just as we used to play and the fact that I was neither emotionally nor physically trained for it meant that the experience was inadequate and that I was trying to recapture something that had been happening in the past. And that seemed morally wrong. Then I witnessed some of the things that were going on in the London scene at that time. There was a bass player, for instance, who by his performance convinced me that he had no idea of what he was doing. I had always been insistent that technically I had to know exactly what I was doing on the instrument. Just achieving the 'general effect' type of playing didn't interest me. And he was doing his fantastic runs and so on and although it sounded in the genre, the appropriate thing in the context, as far as I could see he had no idea what he was doing – he was a clown. He had no conceptual awareness of what he ought to be doing. I thought he was playing a part. And when I realised that it was possible for someone to sham like that it depressed me immensely and I never played my

*own bass again after that. I have played other basses in a number of fairly
undemanding situations but from then on I did no further work on the bass,
and my own bass, which at that time needed repairing, still needs repairing.
Later, after going to America and studying with Cage, and returning here and
joining in, on live electronics, etcetera, some of the playing that was going on
around 1967 and '68 I was becoming more and more ideologically opposed to
improvisation. I began to find improvisation a dead end. I could only get out of
improvisation what I brought into it. But now I come to think of it that wasn't
the case when we played in Sheffield, but later I found more and more with
improvisation – my own improvisation maybe – that I got no more out of it
than I brought to it. I was limited entirely by my own personality and by that of
the people I played with. Unlike the situation in Sheffield, I found the situation
usually produced less than the sum of its parts. It was not possible to transcend
the situation I was playing in.*

*Now on the other hand, I found that by composing I could. Composing, I
could reach conceptions that I could never reach in a limited, defined,
performing time. I couldn't reach an equal conceptual excellence in improvising as in composing. The inadequacy may have been in myself, but, if so, I
transferred it to improvising. In improvisation you could develop a whole
armoury of devices and things you could do and then do them. You might
permutate the order but you were limited to those things you could do. It
could, if you worked very hard, be very sophisticated, but you were always
going to finish up manipulating those things you had developed. The epitome
of that is the skilful jazz player.*

That's right. The whole point of a jazz player's improvisation is that he
works within a clearly accepted and circumscribed idiom. And he accepts these
boundaries, in fact revels in them, because they define his music. Now I would
have though that one of the main things free improvisation provides is the
opportunity to avoid just that situation.

*I had always thought that too, and that's why I admired it and enjoyed
doing it with Joseph Holbrooke. But later I met musicians who gave the lie to
that. I knew they were practising effects during the day and playing them in the
'improvisation' at night. And the call and response type of playing adopted by
so many improvising musicians was unattractive to me. And pieces always
started tentatively, something big in the middle, and then finished quietly.
That sort of arc happened every time. If there are no more formal devices than
that it's pretty empty. Possibly I'm criticising particular improvisors or
particular improvisations.*

In the time you are referring to, the late '60s, there was a lot of confusion
between free improvisation and free jazz. To a lesser extent it still exists. In fact

free improvisation is very often confused in its identity or in its attempt to find an identity. Yet I think there is a type of playing which it is appropriate to describe as free improvisation. But it does seem difficult, firstly to get hold of it, and secondly, to keep hold of it. The tendency is often for the music to slide off into some more readily identifiable area, jazz or comedy or into very obvious forms such as you described. Another aspect of the same problem is that the longer you play in the same situation or group – and this certainly applies to playing solo – the less appropriate it becomes to describe the music as 'free' anything. It becomes, usually, very personalised, very closely identified with the player or group of players. And then you suddenly find yourself in the business of peddling 'my music'. But I believe that that ossifying effect can be counteracted by playing with as many different sorts of improvisor as possible.

One of the main reasons I am against improvisation now is that in any improvising position the person creating the music is identified with the music. The two things are seen to be synonymous. The creator is there making the music and is identified with the music and the music with the person. It's like standing a painter next to his picture so that every time you see the painting you see the painter as well and you can't see it without him. And because of that the music, in improvisation, doesn't stand alone. It's corporeal. My position, through the study of Zen and Cage, is to stand apart from one's creation. Distancing yourself from what you are doing. Now that becomes impossible in improvisation. If I write a piece I don't even have to be there when it is played. They are conceptions. I'm more interested in conception than reality. Because I can conceive of things that don't have any tangible reality. But if I'm playing them, if I'm there at the same time, then that's real. It's not a conception.

A lot of improvisors find improvisation worthwhile, I think, because of the possibilities. Things that can happen but perhaps rarely do. One of those things is that you are 'taken out of yourself'. Something happens which so disorientates you that, for a time, which might only last for a second or two, your reactions and responses are not what they normally would be. You can do something you didn't realise you were capable of. Or you don't appear to be fully responsible for what you are doing. Two examples of this might be the production by some member of the group of something so apt or so inappropriate that it momentarily overwhelms your sensibility – and the results of this type of thing are literally incalculable. Another example, on a totally different time scale, might be Joseph Holbrooke where three people produced over a period of years something they could not have achieved individually or, in fact, could not have expected to achieve collectively. Aren't these things which it is impossible to identify with? Wouldn't this be an example of improvisation producing something not totally determined by the players?

But in the act of the music being made there is no discrimination between the music made and the people making it. The music doesn't exist elsewhere as some general concept.

* * *

The above conversation took place in 1975. Some years later Gavin resumed improvising. In 1991 he described how that came about and gave his current views on improvisation.

My ambivalent feelings about improvisation are still there and some of my conceptual objections to it still remain. In a way my ongoing caveats about improvisation no longer come from a possible hostility between the improvisor and the composer, but rather stem from my perception of difficulties within the activity of improvisation itself. Perhaps the following sequence of events might make this clear.

I have found myself being drawn back into improvisation, little by little, chiefly because of the demands of teaching. Until 1978 I had been teaching in a Fine Art department and so I did not have to confront the question of improvisation as a burning issue in terms of musical practice – although I did even find improvisational painters less interesting to me than those who took a more considered, cerebral approach! But once I started teaching music again, that is dealing with musicians rather than visual artists, in deciding what to teach one of the first things that concerned me was the need to avoid passing on to musicians, or embryo musicians if you like, the kind of difficulties or hang-ups that I'd had as a player or as a composer. That is, my own tastes, my own prejudices which arise from accumulated experience, should not be transmitted to them in such a way that they become their own unquestioned premises. If I was to give a history lecture about a composer for whose work I had little sympathy (I am thinking, for example, of, say, the middle period of Schoenberg, of serial composition, of some aspects of European modernism) then my distaste for some of that music should not be transmitted to the students, at least not at undergraduate level or when they are encountering the music for the first time. I felt that I should discuss the music as it is in itself, and as it was hoped to be received. I could describe it; I could discuss it within a relatively objective framework and say what its merits are within its own terms. Only if I were pressed would I express my own feelings about the music. This 'distant' approach corresponds a little to the way that I was composing during the early 1970s.

But of course some of the student musicians were aware that, in the past, I had been a serious bass player and improvisor and asked me, on occasions, if I would help them with their own work by playing with them. The first instances were when some students were playing transcriptions of jazz solos and wanted a bass player (there were none in the department at the time) to play bass lines. I did help by playing, initially not on my own bass but on a poor college bass (made, I think, of Czechoslovakian plywood). This gave me little sensation of what playing such music was like, but at least it gave the students some experience of being accompanied. I found myself talking about jazz in a historical context too, and I recognised that there were substantial aspects of jazz that had helped form me as a musician and my own repudiation of those should not become part of their thinking. I talked about people like Bill Evans, Lennie Tristano, Ornette Coleman, John Coltrane, Scott LaFaro and others, to put forward the view that their music is as important as any other music of the twentieth century. Little by little I found myself moving more and more towards accepting the music and even taking pleasure in hearing it.

Eventually I found myself playing this music again. I also developed improvisation projects for students, on approaches to 'free' improvisation, and a number of visiting musicians contributed to these projects. I also put improvising musicians into part-time teaching positions. Serious improvisors like Evan Parker and Paul Rutherford began to work as instrumental teachers and, at the same time, help inform the atmosphere of the department. So, for me, improvisation came alive again as an important aspect of a music curriculum, an aspect which I see as academically essential. Musicians should be given the opportunity to encounter improvisation as a serious musical activity and to develop an informed response to it both practically and intellectually, especially where they are being taught by a sceptic. I have also found that more and more, with my own compositional work, the musicians I respect as colleagues or with whom I collaborate are those who have some experience of improvisation, and who are capable of adjusting their playing or of playing with the kind of freedom that I would not get from a musician who is tied exclusively to notation.

My main objections to improvisation have not been eradicated, they have been assimilated into a broader musical practice. The principal conceptual difficulties still remain for me: that of the personalising of music, and of the unity of performer and music. I find it above all uncomfortable to watch improvisors work, and I find recordings of improvisations seldom rewarding. If I have to experience improvisation I would rather it be as a player than from the outside.

CLASSROOM IMPROVISATION

Adapting the only proven effective way of teaching improvisation, the traditional way as exemplified by the Indian method[1], to teaching in a classroom raises many problems: maintaining the necessary degree of empiricism, maintaining the non-documentary, purely practical character of the activity, avoiding the establishment of a set of generalised rules and always allowing an individual approach to develop; these are essentials which, in a classroom situation with, perhaps, a large group of people, are in danger of being lost. And the only places where, to my knowledge, improvisation is successfully taught in the classroom is in those classes conducted by practising improvisors.

In England the first musician to run an improvising class was John Stevens. Stevens has always been a teacher. From the time in the middle 1960s when he emerged as the leading organiser of free music in London, having an idea, for Stevens, has been only a prelude to persuading his friends and colleagues to adopt it. Not surprisingly, his improvisation classes have been successful. Many people who subsequently became regular players have at one time or another attended his classes, many of them meeting each other, and free improvisation, for the first time through him.

He described to me how he came to be teaching improvisation.

I don't know where it started. Something that I often found myself doing long before I started playing free music or almost any music was grabbing people to play, I remember getting together with a brass band cornet player in the army. There was no-one else in the block at that time and I said to him 'come in here and play' and he said 'what shall I play then?' and I said 'play anything you like and I'll drum with it'. He said 'but I can't do that'. And I said 'but you can – just blow a note – any note – and I'll play this and you play that'. And so that was a sort of beginning. And when I teach now it's not that different.

You know I've always been interested in large ensembles. Well, quite often, in order to get one together it would be necessary to have people in the ensemble who, although they were open to playing the sort of music we were playing, would also be professional musicians. I mean that in the bad sense.

---

1 Described in Part One, Indian Music 2 (pages 7-9).

When somebody is a professional musician it often means that his involvement is a bit limited. So, I turned more towards people who were actually getting off on the music but not necessarily playing it. People who were excited by the fact that there was a group of people who were struggling towards some sort of group experience within a free improvisation. These were the listeners and what was required of them would be a real feeling for what was going on. And quite often there were people who were more spirited – more involved in the activity – off the stand than some of those who were on it. There were always people such as the regular members of the Spontaneous Music Ensemble who were totally involved but there might be people playing with us who were less involved.

I remember once in the Little Theatre Club suggesting to the audience that if they wanted to take part there was something they could do in relation to us that was simple and which would create a collective experience within the club. And they did it – and it was a nice experience and some of them, because of hearing us play and because of that experience, started taking up instruments. Their approach to taking up instruments was based on their having listened to us and the way we were playing our instruments so that was the beginning. It was the beginning of people asking me questions and the beginning of me getting involved with people other than developed musicians. Up to then it had always been people like yourself or Evan, developed musicians, people who had gone through other music.

So it started really with the audience at the Theatre Club which actually developed into a group. And because it varied from people who had just started playing to people who had been playing a little longer, then what I would do is get them to do something like – say – inhale deeply, play a long note, as evenly as possible, and get into a collective continuum as a group. Initially, what everyone is looking for is comfort. So if they start on one note and it provides difficulties, they change to something more comfortable. Once they are comfortable with this process of inhaling, exhaling and blowing a note, then they can allow the note to change in sympathy with the group. So that is simple enough for anyone to do. And that includes people using penny whistles, or if they have no instruments, their voices. Another thing that I see as important, in relation to working with groups of people, is staying in touch with the whole group of people all the time. Keeping watch for the equivalent of the little kid at school who is shy – who feels the more things are going on the more he is excluded. And the way I would set up something would always be in direct relationship with that person feeling comfortable. That's a priority. So the method, or process, that you are teaching has to be simple enough to communicate easily to the group as a whole, and for all of them to be able to do *it. But it also has to be demanding enough of concentration to satisfy those who are more developed musicians. So, for instance, in the continuum exercise, the long note thing, the breathing is one part that any musician can concentrate on and find useful.*

Another thing I would use is something else which is basic to people, like numbers. Just counting numbers or using words. Say, for instance, the use of words. A phrase. We'll use the phrase 'a phrase' as an example. If you are going to say 'a phrase' and repeat it, you are going to say it in your own way and it's not so far removed from singing. You're not actually singing, you are saying the words, but in a musical context that can be very close. And because it's simple, when somebody repeats it they realise how close they are to taking part in music. So if you say 'a phrase', accenting the 'a', you have already provided at least a rhythmic element. And that might seem better, more complete, if you say 'a phrase is'. In which case you've improvised.

This thing is so wide and over the years I've developed what you might call pieces and exercises, which do actually work. I don't know how many there are, but it's a lot. They are not written down. I carry them in my head. They are just things that I can use. They are my tools, shall we say. Some of them deal with rhythm, others deal with group involvement, and spontaneity. By that I mean moment by moment involvement. The piece will be designed to require a moment by moment involvement and you are trapped into that. It gives them an experience of how quickly they can relate to each other and forces them to keep their ears open to the rest of the group. So the pieces come out of a need to want to get across a certain experience I might have had. I found the best way to transmit information that I had was to actually do it. I get them to do it in the hope that they will then share my experience of that thing and so know it in the way that I know it. I have this complete faith that if the players can be made to feel a thing working they will then know the essential part about how to do it.

When I go out to do a workshop, though I've been doing it for a long time, as I approach the place there is no real confidence in me about what is going to happen. I always have the same sort of feeling. I can never take it for granted. And walking into the room I'm always apprehensive. And sometimes I wonder 'What am I doing? I'm still doing this and worrying about it.' And there was one period recently which, because of other problems, was particularly hard. And as I travelled towards the place I would think: 'I'll have to give this up. I just don't have that sort of energy any more.' Then I would get there, walk into the room, and there would be about 15 people in there all playing their arses off – great! The impact was just beautiful. And they, the 'pupils', got me there during that time. Then it was easy. The energy came from them.

What's interesting, one of the things that I see as important, is this: I've had to try and avoid a situation where they relied on me to come in and set the whole thing up. I made a rule: I said to them 'You're coming here because you're supposed to want to play. This is a room in which you can play, so, as soon as you get in this room you are going to prove you want to play by getting on and playing. If you don't want to do that, none of what I'm doing here makes any sense whatsoever. If there are four or two or even if you are the first to arrive, as soon as you get here – start playing. And if someone comes who's new to the class then it's the responsibility of the people who are experienced in the class to invite the newcomer to play. In a sense, that is what it is about.' Well, that took a long time to initiate but now there are always people playing together. And now it provides me with a great lift.

The thing about workshops, or improvisation classes, is that you will have some people for, say, three weeks on the trot, and there is something developing. It's becoming almost like a group. Then, a couple of new people will come in. Now, you have to be prepared to let go of the development you have and go wherever the addition of those new people takes it. Whether they can play or not. It's got to go back to a common point.

What I have to keep in touch with at the workshop is a feeling of freedom about playing music, and coupled with that, the feeling of wanting other people to have that same freedom.

Most teaching concerns itself with transmitting a type of proficiency, with imparting a skill, technical ability or know-how. The aim of teaching usually is to show people how to do something. What Stevens aims at, it seems to me, is to instil in the people he works with enough confidence to try and attempt what they want to do *before* they know how to do it. Encouraging them to work empirically, and trusting that they will then learn, with some guidance, from the attempted playing experience.

My object is to incorporate all the people in the room in an experience. A free playing experience. (Relatively free because my presence there as a 'teacher' is always a bit weird.) You get them to apply themselves to this joint experience and some point arrives where we are all 'doing it'. When they walk away from there, that's when the other bit comes in. They are going to examine that experience and try to decide how it happened and what they did to help it happen. And they are going to try and work out how to make it happen again. And the teaching comes in when you provide them with the group experience. Which they provide themselves anyway. And even though this is to do with free playing and it is possible to enter into this without being able to play in tune, or to be able to do anything really, if you are going to continue in music – any kind of music – that group activity experience should be useful to any musical situation you might find yourself in. So it has a general usefulness, I think.

We talked about the non-improvisor and went through the business dealt with in a previous chapter of how the non-improvisor is often a musician who is blocked off from improvising by his training. A training which builds up an attitude towards playing music which prohibits the *attempt* to improvise:

If somebody says to me 'I can't improvise!' – and they could be somebody with the biggest chunk of classical training imaginable in their background – I would find that very inspiring. Because I know that within a very short time they will be doing it and saying 'Oh, is that it?' And then they will do it again. You see, it's the most natural thing in the world.

Subsequently, John Stevens collected his experience of teaching in this way into a book, *Search and Reflect*, which is now used as the basis of all teaching carried out by Community Music of London, who also publish it.

* * *

A musician whose approach to improvising is in many ways totally different to that of John Stevens is the Dutch drummer Han Bennink. For a long time he took, jointly with Misha Mengelberg (his partner in a regular improvising duo), a weekly class in free improvisation. Teaching at a conservatory, the Muziekschool in Haarlem, Holland, meant that the people taught by Han Bennink were, unlike those in John Stevens' classes, trained musicians. We had the following discussion about his approach to teaching them free improvisation.

I do nothing when I go there.

Nothing?

We play records sometimes – say Korean music. Maybe we talk about jazz – how it was. We get them to talk about themselves.

Do you play with them?

Yes, we use those little rules we used to use years ago, you know. Split them into groups – get quiet instruments to play very loud – loud instruments very quiet – play staccato passages – long lines – we use those sort of indeterminate scoring instructions. We used to divide the day into three parts, one part theory, one part analysis, one part playing. Now Misha and I go as the duo – as though we were going to play a gig. We play a little, stop and discuss it, maybe Misha analyses it. Maybe we all talk about it. We keep busy. Everything develops from that. We try and give a little energy to the pupils.

Give energy to the pupils?

I do nothing when I go there. I ask them to think of their own ideas. Any person who is busy with music can think of better ideas than I can. So what I try is to get the ideas coming from the pupils. When it comes to the point that they offer nothing then, of course, I've got some tricks.

Tricks?

If they are not producing anything themselves, then I have some simple statements, some ideas, on which we can work to provoke them, to start them off. For instance, last week I took a radio and turned to the end of the FM scale where you can hear a sort of code, here in Holland. It repeats but after a couple of seconds it's altering – it's that sort of sign, you know. Well, we take that sign and we analyse it, find the notes, the rhythms, and we start to play with it. This week I'll take a kettle with a whistle which, when it boils, produces different pitches in rather an odd, unpredictable way. If it is necessary, we will use that. If it doesn't work out too well you can always say it wasn't your cup of tea.

After a suitable pause, Han returned to the idea:

There you go, it's just the idea – the kettle – certain tones, what's happening with the water and why do you boil water. Is it music and what makes music and what doesn't make music? Examining the idea from every angle – being busy with the idea. That's the whole thing. Looking for each way to come to the middle of it. You can take anything – a piece of paper, a record.

The people Han and Misha teach are either graduates or in their last year at the conservatory, and in addition to being composers and teachers all possess a fairly high level of instrumental ability.

Many of them improvise anyway, you see. Some play the blues or something. Always a borrowed music. Narrow. We try and introduce a broader scale of improvising – as broad as daily life. We are teaching them to make music out of their own background, not someone else's background. Learning what you are. In my eyes that's all you can do. Let people find out what they are and where they are and where their musical influences and preferences come from. Teach them to explore their own background.

It will have become obvious, I hope, that many of the characteristic features of idiomatic improvisation are to be found in free improvisation. In some particulars what can be said about one area of improvisation can be said about all areas. It is true of teaching. The traditional way of learning to improvise – studying with an experienced improvisor in a practical way – joining him in his work – is what is offered to their students by John Stevens and Han Bennink.

123

PART SEVEN

THE LONG-DISTANCE IMPROVISOR

One of a variety of reasons that led me in 1974 to start putting this book together was a suspicion that freely improvised music as an identifiable separate music was finished. Like some early 20th century 'ism', I vaguely felt, it had run its course and would probably continue to exist, if at all, only as some kind of generalised influence. By 1973/4 there had been a noticeable reduction in playing activity and a few defections. And it was around this time that the music was awarded the earliest of its regular obituaries; ill-disguised celebrations which, over the years, have been persistently repeated by those who obviously believe that it should never have happened in the first place.

In fact, this proved to be the start of a period during which the music underwent a considerable expansion. Whereas up until this point the small number of people who played this music not only knew each other but quite regularly played together, now there was an influx of newer players who brought with them a whole range of new musical attitudes and resources.

One group which in some way typified the 'second generation', as they were often called, was Alterations. Although not formed until 1977, all the musicians in it had been around for some time before that – in the case of the percussionist, Terry Day, since the mid-60s – but were identified with 'newer' approaches to playing. The guitarist Peter Cusack formed the group and I asked him how Alterations had come about.

I remember I was living in Holland in 1976, and the group that became Alterations was one of a number I tried at the time. I had no idea that it would do what it did and go on for so long but the reason I settled on that particular one was that I hoped it would sound completely different from other improvising groups then playing. This was because the individuals in it sounded different. Steve Beresford had his tunes and his sense of humour, David Toop, who played an enormous range of flutes at that time which nobody else in the music was doing and Terry Day, the percussionist, who was always very individual in his approach to his instruments. So, I thought it would be different. And it was.

What was the difference?

One of the main differences was that we seemed to have no problem including anything in Alterations – it could be any instrument, a tape of bird song or quotes from any style of music. There was nothing which was taboo.

How is that different from what Han Bennink and Misha Mengelberg were doing at that time?

They were probably a pointer for me. Having just got to Holland, I heard them and other continental groups that I had never come across before. Until then, I didn't know too much about what was happening outside London. However, Alterations took things in its own direction. For example, we started out not using electric instruments although all of us otherwise played them. We then quickly realised that there was no reason why we couldn't include these in improvised music. And so – it just blossomed and everything was included.

One of the ways which struck a listener as a complete departure seemed to be the assumption of a performing environment completely alien to that of most of the improvisation that had gone before – you set up to play as you might in a rock venue – with all that that means – group amplification etc.

That wasn't how it started. But yes, after we started using electric instruments – and there was no conscious decision to do that, everybody just brought more, or different, things along as time went on – there were three electric guitars, a bass, a full drum kit and electric keyboards on stage. We could use, and indeed needed, a PA and were pretty loud at times. It naturally developed in that direction. It sounded like rock music sometimes. Rock venues and rock people were more willing to listen to us than they would to another group of improvising musicians.

Recognisable references had previously been to jazz, new music or electronic music. Alterations introduced other references, popular music, for instance.

I remember at the time quite deliberately wanting to play with Steve and David and Terry because of that. At the start, David's main references were, in fact, based on his knowledge of non-Western musics. Steve's were a whole range of styles, never just any one. Terry was similarly wide-ranging; later on, he often brought his poetry into the group. I was fairly conscious of wanting a group that would take those other areas and use them as improvising references. Another thing was, we had quite a serious attitude towards recording. Everybody, particularly Steve and David, were involved in other sorts of playing and especially those where recording technique was much more of a creative process than just a purely documentary one. The influence of various musical ideas that started life in the studio – dub and reggae techniques, for instance – you can begin to hear in our music. Towards the end we used drum machines and other such devices. So, similar to many in popular musics, we had a strong interest in the relationship between recording techniques and live performance.

There's an obvious connection between Alterations and much improvised music which has happened since – particularly in the U.S.

Pity we weren't from New York.

Some groups continue for ever in some form or other. Why did Alterations finish after 9 years?

We all gradually diverged as people and in our musical interests. I suppose all of us felt that towards the end it just wasn't working as well as it used to. But the actual trigger was the point at which David left and stopped playing live music altogether and, although we didn't discuss it, it became clear that we just didn't want to carry on with a replacement. Alterations was these four people.

* * *

Perhaps it is again necessary to stress that this is an attempt to write about the music, not its history. But these patterns – fluctuations in the visibility of the music, new 'generations' arriving – are part of the way this music has continued.

Another constant feature is the transients, the through-traffic. Those people who come to this kind of playing for a time, find it briefly serves their musical interest, and then take off. There have been quite a few of those.

But most striking is the continuance of those musicians who first appeared with this kind of playing when it claimed an identity for itself twenty-five or so years ago. Virtually all these players, the first generation, have continued to make music in this manner up to the present time.

The ways of survival have sometimes taken odd turns: 'Instant Composition' is, apparently, a broad enough concept to encompass re-arranging the music of Thelonious Monk or Wolfgang Mozart; some players have, at times, been prepared to sit in a big band and play the kind of music that formerly aroused their contemptuous derision, revealing in middle age previously unsuspected jazz 'roots', discoveries which happily coincided with an increase in the popularity of jazz. But these are, probably, simply the kind of manoeuvres sometimes found necessary to safely negotiate the mire thrown up in culturally inclement times.

Then again, it might be that expediency and compromise, the seemingly inevitable tolls exacted by the music industry from those who play music in public, have finally crept into some parts of improvised music. In any event, such deviations are of little consequence. From Paganini to Dizzy Gillespie the most exalted performers of music have at times resorted to all kinds of antics.

Evan Parker, who has maintained at least two continuous musical relationships over many years, one with Paul Lytton in duo, trio and quartet formulations and one as part of the Alex Schlippenbach Trio, points to the musical advantages of continuity.

Things that are established as known between yourselves probably form as useful a context for the evolution of something new as anything. But the inter-personal relationships should only form the basis for working, they shouldn't actually define the music too clearly, which they very often do. In practice, the closest I would get to a laboratory situation is working with the people I know best. It can make a useful change to be dropped into a slightly shocking situation that you've never been in before. It can produce a different kind of response, a different kind of reaction. But the people I've played with longest actually offer me the freest situation to work in.

The really remarkable achievement by the early improvisors, it seems to me, is the survival of the earliest improvising groups. Three of them, MEV, SME and AMM, still function. Their shared taste for acronyms might be a throwback to their formative period, since all these groups began in the mid-60s. With few changes in personnel and with a continuing commitment to their original musical aims all three groups are active more than 25 years later. Holding together an ensemble for a quarter century, as anyone involved in any kind of music will confirm, is a rare achievement. That three of the very small number of improvising groups active in 1966 should still be playing in 1991 might be significant.

Perhaps the most consistent has been AMM. Since 1965 the musicians making up AMM have been Eddie Prevost, percussion; Keith Rowe, guitar; Lou Gare, tenor sax; and Cornelius Cardew, cello. Since Cardew's tragic death John Tilbury, piano and Rohan de Saram, cello have also been regular members. Occasionally other musicians have played with the group but never establishing anything beyond a brief tenure. Twenty six years after its formation it still appears to pursue its original aims with undeviating commitment.

In some way, AMM are the 'official' improvising group, something of an institution. In addition to their longevity, this is partly an acknowledgement of their overt seriousness, a stance not immediately apparent in many improvisors or groups and violently rejected by some. It's a seriousness reflected not only in their playing but in their concern for the philosophical and educational implications of improvised music, articulated in lectures, statements and writings of various kinds. Eddie Prevost, for instance, recently held a post as Visiting Lecturer of Improvisation at the Hull Regional College of Art, is founder-co-ordinator of the 'Improvised Music as an Educational Resource' programme and is currently chairman of AIM – the Association of Improvising Musicians. The following is Eddie's 're-working of material derived from tape-recorded discussions' between us.

At this time (1991), with the re-introduction of Lou Gare to AMM the original three members are now playing together again. This is after Lou's absence of over ten years. Until recently there had never been any duplication of personnel on our dozen or so albums. So our recordings, contrary to the general perception of the ensemble, reflect a constantly shifting membership. Consequently, the music reflects the contributions of each musician and whatever configuration of players is featured.

I'm aware of differences in your group playing since the '60s but that's not surprising, what is surprising is how little it has changed, how little the character of it has changed.

The personalities within the ensemble are clearly defined. They have maintained their integrity. Part of AMM's philosophy, its ethos if you like, is the idea of concurrent commentary: separate voices speaking at the same time, interweaving and interleaving. But each voice is not atomised or individuated. Paradoxically, it may be that individuality can only exist and develop in a collective context. So when the musical situation seems chaotic, when we are caught up in the maelstrom of sound, in which at times it is almost impossible to tell who or what is going on, that is the point when you have to 'distinguish' yourself, delineate your contribution, or else the enterprise is a meaningless cacophony. And, in the final analysis, it's up to each musician to ensure that this does not occur.

Does that explain why it's gone on for over 25 years?

It could. The inner psychology of any long-term ensemble is bound to be complex. We called our 1987 album The Inexhaustible Document. *There is a lot of work to be done. After all, we are part of a movement that has, arguably, remade music. Maybe it's not 'music' according to the convention but it is certainly a new 'sound using' activity; laden with new meanings and cultural implications that differ from what went before. I'm inclined to think of it, at the moment, as a meta-music. One of the generative themes of this meta-music is the relationship between musicians. The music exists and develops through the interchange, the dialogue of the musicians. They set and re-set the agenda – in a continuum. Of course, there are strong feelings between the players – the experience of AMM is perhaps the most important single phenomenon in our lives. (A very un-English kind of statement that). The sharing of such an intense creative experience is in itself instructive. And maybe this psychological inter-action is an important part of the cultural differences that this music offers. We can't blame a composer for making us play such difficult (or banal) music. It's certainly no cosy little club. I doubt if our strong friendships could survive very long without the creative vehicle of AMM. It gives the meaning to our association.*

What seems extraordinary to me is how many people have continued to pursue this activity over such a long time given the lack of economic, or any other kind, of encouragement. AMM, for instance, hasn't been kept together by market forces.

But surely this points to the strength of the music. It is an endless source of intellectual enquiry, inspiration and enjoyment for the musicians – and for the, albeit small, audience that we serve. What more could you ask for? Of course there is no encouragement from those who are in a position to create a more positive environment in which we could work. This is because the music has meanings which do not reflect or celebrate the priorities of the current philosophical/political hegemony. I can't speak for all improvised musics that have arisen in industrial societies (which are, I am sure, qualitatively different from musics arising out of pre-industrial social forms even though they may share certain 'informal' characteristics) and it is impossible, as well as undesirable, to reduce AMM's music to a simple formula. But, there are two dominant generative themes in our work: 'heurism' and 'dialogue'. However, these active, practical ingredients achieve their true significance through investment of meaning and through group and self-definition. The activities of problem-solving within performance and dialogue are techniques which eschew the certainties, the avowed immoveable givens, we are offered upon entry into this life. And this is part of what AMM is about.

Cardew said: '...Training is substituted for rehearsal, and a certain amount of moral discipline is an essential part of this training. In improvisation a kind of training is possible.' Did that translate into anything you specifically did in AMM?

No, they were Cornelius's ideas. Ironically, Cornelius never really engaged in discussions with us about improvising. In fact, he kept out of that to a large extent. I suspect he knew that talk could somehow disturb, or pre-empt, the creative act. But I have always valued what he did say about the way in which he thought AMM was experimental. 'We are searching for sounds and for the responses that attach to them rather than thinking them up, preparing them and producing them. The search is conducted in the medium of sound and the musician himself is at the heart of the experiment.'

And the reasons for the survival, so far, of improvised music in an apparently hostile environment?

Alienation strategies. One thing many of us experienced when we began playing 'free' improvised music was a sense of alienation from the available models – playing models – mainly jazz and classical music. The critical response to what we did was, 'its not jazz'. In some very important sense those remarks were so wrong, but I won't go into that. But irksome though they may have been, those hostile attitudes helped. I suspect that most of us didn't care what it was called, we just wanted to go on playing – and finding out about this new activity in which we were engaged. Being forced to cut what were, in fact, imaginary bonds helped us to recognise our wider cultural and social bearings. It is then that you can begin to calculate where you really want to go. Before, you had been travelling along in someone else's dream. Even if our music began as a negation it seems to have transcended and superseded those earlier formative aspirations – those unfocussed ideas of 'being a jazz musician'. We have gone beyond all that and its attendant imprisoning ethos. This music, of which AMM is a part, goes on, survives and grows. Precisely because it has these reasons for being, these meanings. I get more of an appetite for it as the years go on. I can't think of anything else I would rather be doing.

* * *

The last word on these marathon alliances should go to the Dutch duo, Han Bennink and Misha Mengelberg, a quite different kettle of fish. Lost in the mists of time, its origins are not clear but they are certainly the longest- running of all long-running improvising groups. Of their duo, Misha says:

I would not know what Bennink means with his music, but when our misunderstandings are combined we think that sometimes things are fitting, sometimes complementary. That's maybe a reason for playing duo music. One of the things that inspires me in making any gesture, musically and theoretically, is its relation with daily life in which there is no such thing as an exclusion. One moment I meet you and the next I am washing dishes or playing chess. So many facets on many levels whether you like them or not. Of course, I don't mean daily life transformed into music but in certain respects there are parallels between the music and daily life. For example in the respect that very vulgar things are happening near to very aesthetic things; people go pissing one moment and have deep philosophical thoughts the next. Or maybe both at the same time. Improvisation starts for me at the moment it is needed and it's always in a context in which there are fixed points to refer to. So, the term 'free' is meaningless. The sort of improvisation I am interested in is the sort that everyone does in their lives. They improvise in taking six or seven steps to the door, scratching their heads with one or two fingers. Group improvisation takes place according to common points of education, aims and subjects and is interesting as far as the material reaches. When there is nothing more to develop it should stop.

* * *

These endless sagas are anything but typical. The universal practice in this music, followed by everyone including members of long-lasting groups, is to spend much of their time playing in brief, non-permanent alliances. It is, perhaps, obvious that most casual collaborations should quickly exhaust their areas of mutual interest and consider their common ambitions to be either satisfied or unrealisable. Inevitably, in a music which relies so heavily on invention and for which the feeling of freshness is essential, there is a gradual using up of these resources. At the point when this becomes unmistakable, when the indefinables get defined and the mysteries solved, most groups disband and their members look for fresher, more fruitful alliances. Contact with other musicians and with new musical situations is one of the ways in which improvising musicians look to top up their musical reserves. The tendency is to form a grouping for one or two performances and then re-group, running constant permutations within the available musicians. This, it seems to me, has a natural affinity with free improvisation and, given the diversity of musical approaches that are available, offers a rich resource.

COMPANY

Company seems to have been formed in such a way as specifically to invoke the confrontation of difference and unity. Peter Riley.

It was the increasingly diverse nature of freely improvised music, not its specializations which attracted me and it was in order to take advantage of, to plunder, its expanding resources, that I formed Company. This is how I tried to express it in a programme note for the first Company concert in 1976.

For some time it has seemed to me that the most interesting results in free improvisation come from semi-ad-hoc groupings of musicians ... there is a growing pool of musicians, in England and in other countries, who work together regularly but not continously and not on the basis of being members of a set, permanent group. It is this type of ensemble, not fixed in personnel or style ... which now offers, I believe, the greatest possibilities to be found in free improvisation. Company's structure, such as it is, is based on the idea of the repertory theatre company; a pool of players out of which groupings might be drawn for specific occasions and performances.

There were other, more personal, reasons for forming Company. In this kind of playing I had always found the early stages of a group's development the most satisfying, the most stimulating. Once the music hardens its identity to the point where it becomes susceptible to self-analysis, description and, of course, reproduction, everything changes. The group, having got its act together, discovered 'our music', reaches a stage where, although it might continue to develop musically, and be more marketable – an almost irresistable combination – nevertheless at this point the music becomes less relevant to, less dependent upon, improvisation.

My preference for the early stages of a group's life was something I had been aware of for some years. The Music Improvisation Company, for instance, grew out of a nameless, audience-free situation, to which I would each week invite different musicians. The first one to become a regular was Jamie Muir and gradually the situation evolved into the group described earlier. An almost inevitable process. Once a particular grouping of musicians has played together successfully on a number of occasions the tendency is always, not surprisingly, to turn it into something permanent. But, however strong, almost irresistable, that path is, I came to see it as a deflection from what I wanted to do. So, an important intention in forming Company was to try and establish the 'semi-ad-hoc' procedure as something in itself. Not steps toward either the foundation of a successful group or the abandoning of an unsuccessful one, not some endless search for the perfect combination of musicians, but a recognition that the shifting process itself provided the perfect foundation for making this kind of music.

Inevitably, Company has reflected, sometimes stimulated, the successive changes that have taken place in improvised music, changes which can be seen most clearly in the Company Weeks, which are described below. But since Company's inception the primary aim has remained the pursuit of improvisation as an end in itself: to elevate the method of music-making above its various stylistic results.

* * *

Developing 'semi-ad-hoc' relationships, paradoxically, needs a certain amount of time and an essential part of Company events has always been to have something longer than the single concert situation. This led to the introduction of Company Week.

Company Week is an annual event which has taken place in London since 1977. (In fact, it rarely lasts as long as a week, more usually five days; it is not annual, it didn't happen in '85 and '86 and it has taken place in a number of other cities too, principally New York.) It is self-organised. Five or six concerts on successive evenings for 9 or 10 musicians playing on every concert is the kind of idea that makes music promoters, a notably timid breed, take to the hills. So we – friends, helpers, me – do it.

For the second Company Week in 1978 the programme note read: 'As in 1977 the aim this week is to present free improvisation in a context which is encouraging to the best possibilities in this type of music-making. Company, the collective name for the musicians taking part, was formed for this purpose. It is a pool of musicians of changing personnel whose membership reflects a variety of improvising styles and attitudes. The size and personnel of the groups will be decided by the musicians each night immediately prior to the performance.'

These earlier events in '77 and '78 drew their membership largely from improvisors who, although not sharing formal music-making relationships, would be familiar with, or at least aware of, each other's work. For instance, Leo Smith and Tristan Honsinger, both in the '77 Company Week, had previously worked in quite separate areas but were both improvisors of long experience. Later versions of Company looked to recruit players from virtually any part of the musical spectrum.

134

In '80 and '81 the more theatrical tendencies apparent in improvising circles at that time turned up in Company: a clown, a dancer, performers 'into performance' were sometimes included. It was in this period that the events probably most closely resembled the widely held, completely mistaken, view that free improvisation is a species of chaos: anything goes and nobody cares. A fallacy not shared by anyone with any experience of this activity, as far as I am aware. Company Week 1981, as I remember it (it was recorded, as are most Company Weeks, but there is no technology yet invented which would have adequately documented this particular week) involved lots of water being slung around, the duetting trumpets of Toshinori Kondo and Charlie Morrow extending beyond the confines of the theatre and out into the arms of the London constabulary, and persistent verbal exchanges between the players in half a dozen different languages including gibberish, but throughout this bedlam all the usual self-imposed disciplines and restrictions were present. Occasionally, in fact, someone finds these limits too irksome and makes a dash for total freedom. It never seems to work but people keep trying it. There was a case of this in '81. The Japanese dancer Min Tanaka initiated an experiment in which people simply walked on and off the stage playing wherever, whenever and whatever they chose for as long as they liked. Some hours later (this was an all-day concert) the stage was deserted except for Min, centre stage, trembling with exhaustion. Everybody else, it seemed, was in the bar. If the first discipline of improvisation is spontaneity, as Virgil Thompson claims, then the second might be a sense of what is practical.

In 1982, I started inviting non-improvisors, initially the pianist Ursula Oppens. The sleeve note to *Epiphany*, a record of performances from that week, explains:

...In Company's earlier years the musicians I invited were always from among those who were primarily involved in improvisation although I would usually try to bring together people for whom improvisation served different ends and who were in many cases unfamiliar with each other. The procedure worked well enough, I think, but by 1982 had come to feel just a little cosy. Perhaps this was something we picked up from the stagnant condition of music generally where almost all areas, then as now, share an increasingly enthusiastic commitment to total predictability or maybe it had simply become so commonplace for any improvisor to play with absolutely any other improvisor that differences no longer made any difference. In any event, I had begun to find it useful to invite people who were not primarily, sometimes not at all, involved in improvisation to join us in our improvising. So, for Company Week in 1982, we were ten musicians most of whom had never previously met and some of whom had not previously improvised.

There is, after all, some very basic idea behind 'improvisation': it means getting from A to C when there is no B; it implies a void which has to be filled. Sometimes, in improvising circles, that absence is missing. One way of retaining it was to introduce non-improvisors. My impression is that an improvisor having to deal with a non-improvisor finds it totally different to having to deal with another improvisor, known or unknown. Assumptions have to be dumped, practices usually taken for granted can no longer be relied upon. I also get the impression that it rarely presents much difficulty for a non-improvising musician, working with improvisors, to sort out the various musical signposts, the indications of intent that are common sensory practice. It might take a few days, but it's those few days that I'm interested in.

I don't see the idea of 'progress' as being particularly relevant to what Company does but if the original scheme has developed it is through the range of musical input, the musicians invited, which has widened. Occasionally – in '88 and '90 – there have been much larger events. Company conventions, so to speak, where I invite a much larger number to take part; in 1988 we had 29 people, in 1990 34. But the structure and the intention of the Weeks have remained the same. The time available, the way of choosing the groups, the musicians invited: all are designed to remove as far as possible any preconceptions as to what the music might be, to make improvisation a necessity, and keep it at the forefront of the activity.

* * *

The assembling of a Company Week – who I invite – is neither haphazard nor meticulously planned and to some extent the choice of musicians might simply reflect the people I have worked with over the preceding period.[1] But there are many exceptions to this and sometimes it takes a long time to get the right people in the right place at the right time. I might keep somebody in mind for a long time before actually inviting them to a particular event and that will only be when the relationship between them and the other players on that event, the degree of unfamiliarity and the potential for compatibility, seem right. Except, it's not quite as straightforward as that. Sometimes a wild card can be very effective.

Company is about mutual music-making and, at times, demands the sacrifice of individual preferences. It calls for musical generosity, curiosity and sensitivity, the ability to respond instinctively and constructively to new and

---

1 I've found writing about Company the most difficult part of putting this book together. The Weeks particularly are emotional, musically intoxicating experiences; pretty much my ideal way of working. Any kind of objective analysis is very remote from my relationship with these events so I am particularly obliged to John Fordham, Chris Blackford and Kenneth Ansell for their suggestions and the use of interview material in this chapter.

unfamiliar situations. The people I invite are more often than not highly individual players, distinctive in instrumental styles and artistic attitudes, so it is a source of continuing amazement and gratitude to me that the commitment and enthusiasm with which they pursue these projects is virtually always total and unreserved. Whatever the initial difficulties and in spite of the obvious risks, once the process is underway people seem to become immersed in it, almost taken over by it.

There is an intimacy about this process – building music through group improvisation – which, as it develops, demands a kind of surrender. Not too many people have the courage, or the humility perhaps, to talk about these things; the singer Vanessa Mackness does. Of taking part in Company she said:

You have to be prepared to take risks. Sometimes I feel that I've made a terrible fool of myself. But then I think, no, you have to be prepared for that. I think you gradually develop a way of saying less. I think the more mature musicians really have a sense of that. Maybe you could hear that in the last piece we played tonight. Everybody waited and built the piece gradually. That really does take maturity. It also requires patience both from the musicians and the audience.

For me the whole thing was a very profound experience, the problems, the development, the creative struggle, everything. The reality of everyone's role, everyone's humanity. I shall never forget it. It has fortified me and helped me grow.

Leo Smith, who took part in some of the earliest events, looks at it like this:

Whenever I play with Company I play the music of Company. It's not my music as you would otherwise hear it. I would not choose this medium to totally dominate my creative output but it's nice to come together and deal with other aspects of creative music.

Company Week 1984, which, the programme note says, featured musicians '...from different parts of the musical universe who in some cases are completely unfamiliar with each other's work', included two non-improvisors – Anthony Pay, who appears earlier in this book discussing being a non-improvisor, and also Philip Eastop, the horn player, at that time working with the London Sinfonietta. About playing on that Week, Philip said:

I suppose I was a bit nervous at first because I'd never sat in front of an audience before without a piece of printed music in front of me. And although I kept saying to myself 'Look, this is what you've always wanted to do', when it came to doing it, I was quite worried about it. Then once it came to playing, it was just like being given a pair of wings; it was an incredibly liberating experience – at last I could play what I wanted.

He then described the difficulties he encountered as he exercised that liberty:

On the first night I was in two or three pieces and I used up all my general ideas, like double-stopping, lip trills and certain kinds of sounds. By the second night, I had to start repeating them and by the third night I wished I'd been a bit more sparing with them. Then I thought 'Am I being spontaneous in working in that way?' The difficulty is knowing how to approach improvising. And I had to evolve, very quickly, a new way of listening. I was never sure whether to play with people, against them, or to react to them... I think I tried everything.

* * *

At the present time of writing, in the period immediately following Company Week 91, I am still under the influence of that event, marvelling at how beautifully it worked. Not at how good or bad the music was – much of the playing was very fine indeed – but simply at how it had taken place, the alchemy which had produced it.

The violinist Alexander Balanescu was one of the musicians who took part. When he was interviewed by Chris Blackford about his experiences in Company Week 91 he said:

It's a great adventure. It's also a learning process for me. Every night I find things out about myself as well as the other musicians. It gives me a lot of strength. This is quite a difficult thing for a classically trained musician to be doing. You don't have the music to hide behind, you are very much on the line. After each night I feel a sense of achievement because I've gone through it and managed to express something.

Two American musicians taking part in the same Week were the improvisor/composer/saxophonist John Zorn and the rock guitarist Buckethead. About working with them Balanescu said:

Tonight's concert was very entertaining, there was a lot of variety and humour. I found it interesting working with John Zorn who works in this filmic way, with things changing very quickly. On the other hand, somebody like Buckethead stays on one thing for quite a long period of time.

When asked about Buckethead's volume level, described as 'loud, agressive and dominating', Balanescu said:

Yes, but I find that it's quite lyrical as well as being aggressive. He's always playing melodies and it's interesting to contrast him with Derek who's much more of a textural player. I think it's great that all these different personalities have the opportunity to come together.

Asked if his classical background was of any use in this improvising context he said:

Yes, it is. If I try to observe my own mental process when I'm improvising, all kinds of memories of things one's heard surface. I don't try to exclude any influence.

Yves Robert, the virtuoso French trombonist, experienced in jazz, theatre, film and freely improvised music, also took part in the '91 Company Week. He said:

Playing improvised music is like writing without a pen. It demands great concentration to hear everything that is happening from other musicians and at the same time to be playing yourself. You also have to be able to remember what has happened the second before and the minute before and so keep in mind the shape of what's happening, how the piece is being constructed. It all depends on the people you are improvising with. Sometimes they have a very different way of working to yourself. Sometimes it might work perfectly and at other times there's too much happening. Obviously you have to adapt your way of playing depending on who you are working with.

In music, strangely, adventurousness seems to be a rare commodity. And yet, it is the one characteristic shared by all of the many different kinds of players who have taken part in Company. Perhaps it is a quality which is generated, or released, by improvisation. In any event, year after year these groups of very special individuals have taken my invitation and have collectively transformed it into unique music which, never less than worthwhile, has been at times truly remarkable.

LIMITS AND FREEDOM

In 1987, seven musicians, all closely associated with improvisation, took part in a public discussion staged as an adjunct to a series of concerts.[1] Inevitably, the first subject up for consideration concerned the relationship between improvisation and composition. After forty minutes of collective incoherence and mutual misunderstandings, the predominant view to emerge was that there is no such thing as improvisation, or, if there is, it is indistinguishable from composition. Furthermore, composition, should there be such a thing, is no different to improvisation. Having established that, there didn't seem to be anything else to discuss and the group dispersed, gratefully returning to playing music: improvising, in fact.

This, in a sense, is where we came in. Improvisation is not a word which is highly thought of, particularly by improvisors, some of whom will go to considerable lengths to avoid being tarred with what they have found to be an unhelpful brush. But, additionally, there was a view struggling to be expressed which is, I think, a fundamental belief for some people: musical creativity (all creativity?) is indivisible; it doesn't matter what you call it, it doesn't matter how you do it. The creation of music transcends method and, essentially, the composition/improvisation dichotomy doesn't exist.

This kind of spongy generalisation often obscures, perhaps by design, more than it reveals but, pushed to its limits, it still can't hide the fundamental difference that separates composition and improvisation. In any but the most blinkered view of the world's music, composition looks to be a very rare strain, heretical in both practice and theory. Improvisation is a basic instinct, an essential force in sustaining life. Without it nothing survives. As sources of creativity they are hardly comparable.

None of these lofty projections, however, are necessary to reveal the manifest and multiple differences between composition and improvisation. Here's one, for instance, discovered at street level by composer/improvisor Frederic Rzewski and improvisor/composer Steve Lacy. Frederic tells the story:

---

1 This took place at the BIM House in Amsterdam. The musicians involved were: Cecil Taylor, John Zorn, George Lewis, Misha Mengelberg, Butch Morris, Gerry Hemingway and me. The transcribed results eventually appeared in *Jaarboek 7* published by Van Gennep, Amsterdam.

In 1968 I ran into Steve Lacy on the street in Rome. I took out my pocket tape recorder and asked him to describe in fifteen seconds the difference between composition and improvisation. He answered: 'In fifteen seconds the difference between composition and improvisation is that in composition you have all the time you want to decide what to say in fifteen seconds, while in improvisation you have fifteen seconds.'

His answer lasted exactly fifteen seconds and is still the best formulation of the question I know.[2]

* * *

These discussions are conducted only, I think, within the world of freely improvised music and arise from the contradiction inherent in attempts to organise or to combine composition and 'free' improvisation. Other areas of improvisation – 'idiomatic' – combine fixed and improvised naturally enough, both working organically from a common base. Perhaps the nearest thing to a successful combination of fixed and freely improvised music is in the long serving improvising groups where, as Evan Parker admits, 'I think we accepted long ago those aspects of each other's playing that we are never going to be able to change and we work upon the parts that are negotiable'.

The debates, of course, are unimp   fact, external matters – aesthetics, musical fashion, even econ   unique degree irrelevant to the practice of this kind of m   eems to be no apparent correlation between the v   ity of improvisation. Its survival, its general heal   rected by the shifting security of its precarious toehold   opes of the music industry. There are now, to be sure, a numb   vising virtuosi operating on the fringes of one or other of the esta   ed music markets, and U.S. improvisors particularly have conducted a sustained assault on the outskirts of rock, but in virtually all cases where some kind of uneasy alliance with the wider music world has been achieved the improvisor's function amounts to little more than peripheral decoration, accepted, if at all, for its novelty value. The bulk of freely improvised music, certainly its essential part, happens in either unpublicised or, at best, under-publicised circumstances: musician-organised concerts, ad hoc meetings and private performances. In other words, simply in response to music-making imperatives. And it's easy to see that the more conducive the setting is to freely improvised music, the less compatible it is likely to be with the kind of presentation typical of the music business.

2 From 'Listen to Lacy', a brochure published by Wiener Musik Galerie in 1990 to accompany a series of concerts.

Speculations about the future of free improvisation – its possible popularity or extinction – seem to me totally to misunderstand the function of the activity. Rather like presuming that the course of the sun is affected by the popularity of sun-bathing. It is basically a method of working. As long as the performing musician wants to be creative there is likely to be free improvisation. And it won't necessarily indicate a particular style, or even presuppose an artistic attitude. As a way of making music it can serve many ends.

Paradoxically, and in spite of the earlier arguments, it seems to me now that in practice the difference between free improvisation and idiomatic improvisation is not a fundamental one. Freedom for the free improvisor is, like the ultimate idiomatic expression for the idiomatic improvisor, something of a Shangri-la. In practice the focus of both players is probably more on means than ends. All improvisation takes place in relation to the known whether the known is traditional or newly acquired. The only real difference lies in the opportunities in free improvisation to renew or change the known and so provoke an open-endedness which by definition is not possible in idiomatic improvisation. And this is certainly a great enough difference, but in its moment to moment practice the essentials of improvisation are to be found, it seems to me, in all improvisation, and its nature is revealed in any one of its many forms.

In all its roles and appearances, improvisation can be considered as the celebration of the moment. And in this the nature of improvisation exactly resembles the nature of music. Essentially, music is fleeting; its reality is its moment of performance. There might be documents that relate to that moment – score, recording, echo, memory – but only to anticipate it or recall it.

Improvisation, unconcerned with any preparatory or residual document, is completely at one with the non-documentary nature of musical performance and their shared ephemerality gives them a unique compatibility. So it might be claimed that improvisation is best pursued through its practice in music. And that the practice of music is best pursued through improvisation.

I believe the above to be true. But improvisation has no need of argument and justification. It exists because it meets the creative appetite that is a natural part of being a performing musician and because it invites complete involvement, to a degree otherwise unobtainable, in the act of music-making.

BIBLIOGRAPHY

Adyonthaya, Shri N.M., *Melody Music of India*, Mangalore 1965

Arnold, F.T., *The Art of Accompaniment from a Thorough-bass*, Oxford University Press 1931

Blackford, Chris, *Rubberneck 9*, Basingstoke 1991

Canetti, Elias, *Crowds and Power*, London 1962

Cardew, Cornelius, 'Towards an Ethic of Improvisation', *Treatise Handbook*, Edition Peters, London

Cauldry, N., 'Turning the Musical Table – Improvisation in Britain in 1965-1990', *Contemporary Music Review*, Harwood Academic Publishers 1991

Clifton, Thomas, 'Comparison between Intuitive and Scientific Descriptions of Music', *Journal of Music Theory* 1976

Dean, R, *New Structures in Jazz and Improvised Music since 1960*, Open University Press 1991

Danielou, Alain, *The Situation of Music and Musicians in the Countries of the Orient*, International Music Council 1971

Dupré, Marcel, *Cours Complet d'Improvisation a l'Orgue*, Paris 1925 (2 volumes)

Ferand, E.T., *Die Improvisation in der Musik*, Zurich 1938

Ferand, E.T., 'The Howling in Seconds of the Lombards', *Musical Quarterly*, July 1939

Ferand, E.T. (ed), *Improvisation in Nine Centuries of Western Music*, Cologne 1961

Fischer, Ernst, *The Necessity of Art* (1959), Penguin 1963

Gangoly, O.C., *Ragas and Raginis*, np nd

Globokar, V., *Komposition und Improvisation*, Breitkopf & Hartel, Wiesbaden 1977

Grace, Harvey, *The Complete Organist*, London 1920

Hamilton, A., 'The Aesthetics of Imperfection', *Philosophy*, July 1990

Heinichen, J.D., *Der General-Bass in der Composition* (1728), ed G.Buelow, University of California 1966

Koestler, Arthur, *The Roots of Coincidence*, Pan Books 1974

Kofsky, F., *Lenny Bruce*, Monad 1974

Lambert, Constant, *Music Ho!*, London 1936

Lewis, G., *Phenomenology,* unpublished thesis 1979

Lucas, Clarence, *Musical Form,* London 1905

Matheson, J., *Kleine General-Bass Schule,* 1735

Microphone (percussion issue), London June 1972

Moszkowski, Alexander, *Conversations with Einstein,* London 1921

Nettl, B., 'Thoughts on Improvisation', *Musical Quarterly* 60, 1-19. 1974

Pressing, J., *Improvisation: Methods and Models,* Oxford University Press 1985

Pressing, J.,*Cognitive Processes in Improvisation,* La Trobe University 1984

Sachs, Curt, *The Wellsprings of Music,* London 1944

Sachs, Curt, *The Rise of Music in the Ancient World, East and West,* New York 1943

Sartre, Jean-Paul, *Sketch for a Theory of the Emotions,* London 1971

Schouten, H., *Improvisation on the Organ,* Paxton, London 1955

Smith, Herman, *The World's Earliest Music,* London 1902

Smith, Leo, *Notes: 8 pieces,* Hamden 1973 (see p.84)

Srinivasan, R., *Facets of Indian Culture,* Bombay 1970

Stevens, J., *Search & Reflect,* Community Music, London

Stewart, Rex, *Jazz Masters of the Thirties,* London 1972

Wachsmann, K., *The Changeability of Musical Experience,* Society for Ethnomusicology, Inc. 1982

Westrup, J., *Musical Interpretation,* BBC, London 1971

Whitmer, T.C., *The Art of Improvisation,* New York 1934

Williams, D., *The Improvisor* (magazine). 6 Glen Iris Park, Birmingham, Alabama, USA

Zonis, Ella, *Classical Persian Music,* Harvard UP 1973

These are some of the books and articles I looked at, a number of which are mentioned in the text. There has been a substantial increase in recent times in writings dealing with improvisation. Recordings of improvising musicians discussing their work, perhaps a more promising source of information, are also increasingly available. In Britain, the National Sound Archive has an extensive reference library, and a wide range of recorded interviews which are available for public listening.

examining the idea from every angle - being busy with the idea. That's the whole thing. Looking for each way to come to the middle of it **Han Bennink** I've always tried to provoke the musician to go beyond his habits **Earle Brown** the accidental, the chaotic. You know, the stuff that you can't control or you can't predict **Jerry Garcia** it's something that should be heard, enjoyed or otherwise, and then completely forgotten **Stephen Hicks** when you start to play off the top of your head, that's when the truth is really known about people **Steve Howe** a musician is trying to use whatever liberty he has within the raga to extend the limits of that raga without destroying its basic features **Viram Jasani** the most important thing for an improvisor is to be able to think quickly **Jean Langlais** it started from what we accept as silence. And every move meant something **Tony Oxley** the violinists, and the other string players in the group, spurred the harpsichordist on...the harpsichordist might then think of something first and they would follow him **Lionel Salter** an improvisor wants to have the freedom to do anything at any time **John Zorn** the basic characteristic of music-making is improvisation **Derek Bailey**

Born in Sheffield, Derek Bailey studied music with C.H.C.Biltcliffe and guitar with, amongst others, George Wing and John Duarte. Throughout the 1950s he worked as a guitarist in every kind of musical situation - clubs, concert halls, radio, TV and recording studios. He became increasingly interested in the possibilities of a freely improvised music and by the mid-60s was devoting himself exclusively to this field. He has performed solo concerts in all the major cities of Europe, Japan and North America, played with most of the musicians associated with free improvisation, and recorded over 90 albums on labels including CBS, RCA, Deutsche Grammophon and Island.

In 1970, along with Tony Oxley and Evan Parker, he founded Incus Records, the first independent, musician-owned record company in Britain. In 1976 he established Company, a changing ensemble of improvising musicians drawn from many backgrounds and countries that performs throughout the world. In 1977 an annual Company Week was inaugurated in London. He now divides his time between solo performances, organising and playing in Company events, running Incus, practising, writing and – something he considers essential – ad hoc musical activities.

Improvisation: its nature and practice in music was originally written in 1975/6 and first published in 1980. Translations followed in Italian, French, Japanese, Dutch and German, and it has formed the basis of a series of TV films made by Jeremy Marre and screened in several countries in 1992.